ARIEL

Ariel

JOSÉ ENRIQUE RODÓ

Translation, Reader's Reference,
and Annotated Bibliography by
MARGARET SAYERS PEDEN

Foreword by James W. Symington
Prologue by Carlos Fuentes

UNIVERSITY OF TEXAS PRESS, AUSTIN

Tenth paperback printing, 2008

Requests for permission to reproduce material from
this work should be sent to:
Permissions
University of Texas Press
P.O. Box 7819
Austin, TX 78713-7819
utpress.utexas.edu/index.php/rp-form

LIBRARY OF CONGRESS
CATALOGING-IN-PUBLICATION DATA
Rodó, José Enrique, 1871–1917.
  Ariel.
  Bibliography: p.
  Includes index.
  I. Title. II. Series.
PQ8519.R6A713   1988   864   87-19202
ISBN 978-0-292-70396-4 (pbk.)

Contents

Foreword

"May the genius of Uruguay which produced *Ariel* guide our thoughts." Thus spoke President Otto Arosemena of Ecuador in his keynote address to the Conference of American Presidents in Punta del Este, Uruguay, in April 1967. As U.S. chief of protocol I sat with the delegation headed by President Lyndon Johnson. "Ariel" was a familiar memory. I had learned the part for a grammar school production of *The Tempest*. But Shakespeare was hardly Uruguayan. Who, then, was this "genius" who had usurped "Ariel?" I asked the members of President Johnson's staff. They knew not. I went over to the press table where the literati were gathered and put the question to them. "Forget it," was the response of perspiring journalists waiting impatiently for the "bottom line" numbers in aid and trade. The opening line of a keynote address seemed to deserve better. The reaction brought to mind the fellow who was asked: "Which is worse, ignorance or apathy?" and replied, "I don't know and I don't care."

But when my circle of inquiry included an Uruguayan diplomat, the answer came quickly. *Ariel,* he told me, was an essay written at the turn of the century by the Uruguayan philosopher José Enrique Rodó and "well known" to students of Latin American literature and thought. Copies were probably available, he said, in the nearest bookstore. He was right. I still have the dog-eared paperback Spanish edition that I bought that afternoon and took to the beach for a quiet read.

Maybe it was the approaching dusk and the stillness after the bustle and babble of the plenary session. Perhaps it was the solitude and the room it made in my mind for the author's gentle message. But speaking over the chasm of years with confidence and wisdom, his "Prospero," surrounded by a few admiring students, seemed, in fact, to be addressing a much wider audience, including generations to come—and most particularly our own.

By "our own" I mean the "me generation" of today, whose cultural retardation is the subject of the two best-sellers in nonfiction at this writing, E. D. Hirsch's *Cultural Literacy* and Allan Bloom's *The Closing of the American Mind*. Each holds a distinctive mirror up to the emerging life of America's young people, and the reader recoils from the images of minds and ambitions untethered to inspiring memory and "artificially restrained from the enthusiasm for high virtue."

Yet it was in neither of these timely critiques that the following observations appeared :

A civilization acquires its character
not from a display of prosperity or material supremacy,
but from the grandeur of thought and
feeling possible within it.

. . . we must begin by recognizing that when
democracy is not ennobled by an idealism
equally as energetic as the society's material
concerns, it will inevitably lead to a
favored status for mediocrity.

Now that barbarism no longer unleashes
its often heroic and regenerative hordes to
attack the beacons of civilization, high culture
must be on its guard against the mild but
equally destructive effect of different peaceful,
even educated, hordes: the inescapable hordes
of vulgarity.

These reflections appear, rather, in *Ariel,* written before airplanes, TV, and microchips by a young man of twenty-nine who foresaw with clarity and sadness the encroachment of "utilitarianism" on the world's technically advanced societies. Thus, while cognizant and respectful of North American achievements in political freedom, science, and technology he, in effect, urges the youth of Hispanic America not to become "de-Latinized" in their emulation of the North; hence, the suggested association of the United States with Caliban as distinct from that reverence for beauty and its derivatives, justice and morality, that were implicit in *Ariel* and that he pled with his "students" to retain. We should not be too quick to take offense—in part because some, not all, of his criticisms are valid, and in part because he did not intend to single out the United States, but rather to use it as a convenient model for the analysis of a problem he saw advancing on all humanity.

Not that he was or is universally acclaimed by Latin American contemporaries and successors. He is faulted severally for elitism, for inattention to the Amerindian contribution to Spanish America's cultural development, and for appearing to idealize a state of repose in societies in need of hard work. A reading of Carlos Fuentes' spirited introduction provides ample evidence of the ambivalence that characterizes the judgments of Rodó's peers. Were there an "Encyclopedia Hispánica," the Rodó article would be quite a challenge for the editors. The current edition of the Britannica notes that Rodó is "considered by many to have been Spanish America's greatest philosopher." The edition available to the U.S. participants in our 1967 summit gathering attributed his influence as "a rallying point of Latin American youth" to "his authority as exponent of optimism, as stylist and as advocate of unity in Spanish American literature and culture . . . hailed by Spanish Americans as their philosopher par excellence."

Here certainly was sufficient notice to a delegation of North

Americans presumably seeking common ground with their Latin counterparts. Perhaps it could be said, in paraphrase, "the bigger they are, the harder it is to get their attention." In a recent commentary Fuentes noted, "For the people of North America to truly understand the political phenomena of Latin America, they must first understand its cultural identity. . . . Democracy in Latin America is fragile, and must come from a Latin American reality, not in spite of it."

Had he been present to prompt the U.S. actors at the 1967 summit he would have caught the significance of the keynoted *Ariel,* and perhaps culled heartening references from it to adorn President Johnson's response. It was Rodó who saw his North American neighbors as "the first to evoke our modern ideal of liberty, forging" it into "imperishable bronze and living reality." It was Rodó who defended the duality of America inherent "in the classic myth of the two eagles released simultaneously from the two poles in order that each should reach the limits of its domain at the same moment." After a flight of eighty-eight years the eagle-borne thoughts of Rodó may have reached our airspace. Shall we guide them in or shoot them down? Is it true that the "gods have departed"? Is "otium" essential? Reasonable minds can differ, and in the higher realms of academe have differed, on the validity of Rodó's biases, his assumptions, and his message. But as far as the general public is concerned, every school of thought on these questions has been on vacation.

It was with all this in mind that I proposed the project of a new edition. It required a new translation, an introduction, and a publisher. Fortune smiled on every need. Margaret Sayers Peden of the University of Missouri produced the translation with clarity, sensitivity, and elegance; Carlos Fuentes has provided an introduction of challenging insight, ardor, and perspective; the publisher? One of the foremost names in the publication of Hispanic American studies. *Ariel* should be read by students in this country between the ages of eighteen and eighty, who will plunge undaunted into the often complex references and trace even the most obscure to their rewarding sources, students withal who will be inclined to ponder at least the assertion that "one day of public life in Attica offered a more brilliant program of instruction than any we draw up in our modern institutions."

For I look to the time when today's children, the fathers and mothers of tomorrow's leaders, will be well prepared for that journey beyond our domains, where exchanges of hope and insight can occur with a shared sense of the past, its pain and its promise. In this great hemisphere of promise, this still-new world, we, the co-descendants of discovery, will soon mark the half-millennium that has conjoined our fates since the *Santa María* made port at Dominica. To do justice to that commemoration will require a grand opening—of the minds and hearts of all Americans. To help us cross that threshold with confidence and serenity we could do worse than reach for Rodó, the letters of whose name, more easily rearrangeable than our priorities, spell "Door."

What lies beyond—mutual respect and reciprocity between North and South? That would indeed be Rodó's "America we dream of." Will it be ours? As we decide, his spirit hovers with a kind of Promethean patience. And should we look up, we, like the awestruck student at the close of *Ariel*, may notice something "descending from above upon these indifferent masses."

JAMES W. SYMINGTON
Washington, D.C.
June 1987

Prologue

I

This is a supremely irritating book. In Spanish, its rhetoric has become insufferable. Rodó belonged to the *modernista* movement, which sought a cosmopolitan atmosphere for Latin American poetry, cultivated art for art's sake, and affected an accompanying languor, elegantly settled into the semirecumbent position of turn-of-the-century ennui. The influence of French Symbolism and Parnassianism was all-important to the *modernistas*. Their poetical genius transformed the poetry written in the Spanish language from within Spanish America, radically altering the habits of writing in Spain itself. The greatest of the *modernista* poets—the herald and hero of the movement—was the Nicaraguan Rubén Darío, of whom it was said that he had sent the galleons back to Spain. Darío could affect the greatest preciosity, but also concentrate on the starkest poetic statement, as in "Lo fatal," one of the clearest and most beautiful poems ever written in Latin America, or soar away into political bravura, as in his poems on Theodore Roosevelt, Walt Whitman, and the Spanish language.

Rodó is not a poet and his range is not Darío's. He is an orator. He does not invent the rhetoric of *modernismo;* he uses it in a particular twilight setting. He is twenty-nine when he writes *Ariel,* but he poses as an elderly teacher, surrounded by his disciples and delivering his philosophical testament. This valetudinarian stance does not preclude the rhetorical flourishes of what is basically a written speech. The *orator* suddenly flies away toward the *oratorio:* a bizarre kind of musicality is achieved, as though of Greek goddesses dancing to Elgar's *Pomp and Circumstance.*

I recall that, in the forties and fifties, oratorical contests were still in vogue throughout Latin America and, certainly, in Mexico. I went to hear them out of some kind of educational yet sensual need: a warning to myself, with a dash of masochism. It was rare for the tremulous orators of our youth not to quote Rodó in their speeches: the topics of the spiritual versus the utilitarian, blithe Latin American Ariel fighting off brutish North American Caliban, beauty confronting ugliness, followed by a whole parade of simplistic dualisms (vulgar versus delicate, good versus evil, and so on) were facile, tempting devices for the young lawyer, politician, or journalist on the rostrum. And Rodó had wrapped *Ariel* in such a glowing sycophancy of youth! Bathed in virtue, the young orator appeared to prolong the puzzling fame of José Enrique Rodó.

Why Rodó, then? Why *Ariel?*

The English-language reader, let me hasten to say, is privileged. He is reading Margaret Sayers Peden's superb translation, which, while being perfectly faithful, simply finds more neutral equivalents to some of Rodó's excesses, eliminates long sentences and subordinate clauses in favor of shorter phrases that say exactly the same things written by Rodó, and, in general, immerses the text in a kind of Erasmian serenity that contains a hint of Rodó's madness but denies it the pitfall of rhetorical madness. The folly is there, all right, and it should not be lost. But it is no longer a rhetorical folly; it is the folly of urgent communication; it starts to explain, thanks to Peden's lucidity as a translator, why the insufferable Rodó and his moth-eaten *Ariel* matter.

I stand by what I say: the bilingual reader may compare the Caliph's legend as written by Rodó in Spanish to Peden's English version on pages 45–47. She makes it sound as mysterious and beautiful as a tale by Borges. Rodó wrote it as garishly as a Universal film of the Arabian Nights starring María Móntez.

But along with my complaints, the question stands: Why Rodó, why *Ariel,* after all this time, after all this rhetoric he inflicted upon us while tickling our aesthetic fancies, our political indulgences, and youthful vanities? Why?

II

Ariel is an essential book in the protracted Latin American search for identity. It is set exactly at the middle of our independent life. It appears in 1900, in the wake of the poetic revolution of the *modernistas,* which came to an end with the First World War. As we now reach the year 2000, we can look back on 1900—the year of *Ariel*—with a certain perspective, and it is the following:

Spanish America broke away from Spain between 1810 and 1821, and the break was not only political, but moral and aesthetic as well. For most liberals, independence meant renouncing the Spanish past as a reactionary, intolerant, and unscientific era of darkness. It meant promptly attempting to recover lost time by achieving all that the Spanish Counter-reformation denied us: capitalism, free inquiry, free speech, due process, parliamentarism, industry, commerce: in short, modernity. This was to be by legal *fiat.* It sufficed to copy the progressive legislation of France, England, and the United States. Democracy and prosperity would follow.

It was not to be so. The real country festered behind the legal country, the vacuum between law and reality was too vast, and the Latin American tyrant—Santa Anna in Mexico, Rosas in Argentina, Francia in Paraguay—rushed in to fill it. The pro-Spanish, conservative intelligentsia defended tradition and saw the greatest danger to Spanish America in the expansion of the

United States, capitalist, Protestant, populist, opposed to privilege and bearer of the glad tidings of democracy. For these same reasons, the liberals were the enthusiastic admirers of the United States. But when the territorial ambitions of the North Americans, their self-justifying messianism (Manifest Destiny) and self-serving thesis (the Monroe Doctrine, forbidding Latin America what the United States had egregiously profited from during its Revolutionary War, namely, European help), actively expressed themselves in the war of 1847, which deprived Mexico of Texas, New Mexico, Arizona, Colorado, Nevada, California, and parts of Utah and Oregon, the United States became the Jekyll and Hyde of our wildest continental dreams: a democracy inside, an empire outside.

Spain, our old empire, was defeated and dismantled by the United States, our new empire, in 1898; the Philippines and Puerto Rico became North American colonies, Cuba a subject state. Our sympathies shifted to the defeated empire: the United States desatanized Spain while satanizing itself. Walker's takeover in Nicaragua, the mutilation of Colombia so that the Panama Canal could be held independently of Latin America, intervention in Mexico in 1914 and again in 1917, Marines in Haiti, Honduras, Nicaragua, and the Dominican Republic. In the center of the period stretching between Manifest Destiny and the Good Neighbor Policy, Rodó's *Ariel* appears as the emotional and intellectual response of Latin American thought and Latin American spirituality to growing North American imperial arrogance, gunboat diplomacy, and big stick policies.

This book must be placed in order to be understood. Its intellectual option is French-oriented, because France, in the nineteenth century, came to represent the equilibrium we needed in our stormy tug-of-war between allegiance to Spain and allegiance to the United States. Paris gave us culture without strings and a sense, furthermore, of elegance, disinterestedness, wholeness, aristocracy, and links to the culture of the clas-

[16]

sics, sorely lacking in the vagabond, unrooted, homogenizing pioneer culture of the United States or in the monastic, far-too-rooted, isolated culture of Spain. El Escorial and La Mancha, the Mississippi River and the covered wagon, could not compete with the symmetry of the gardens, the thoughts, and the laws of France: Versailles, Descartes, and the Napoleonic Code.

The Parisian perfume is at times almost faint-provoking in Rodó. To read him in this light, nevertheless, is useful as a reminder of fleeting glories. Rodó quotes admirably and admiringly from French authors that hardly anyone, even in France, remembers today: Baudet, Guyau, Rod, Jules Lemaître, Téodor de Wyzewa. The more durable French authors—Renan, Michelet, Baudelaire—are not sufficiently enriched by contrasting galaxies. Rodó finds the exceptions to North American grossness in Poe and Emerson, but his expressed dismissal of the literature of the United States is all the more difficult to swallow *in absentia* of Melville, Hawthorne, James, Emily Dickinson, and Walt Whitman.

Even worse is his practical exclusion of Spanish and Spanish American authors, as if only France held the keys to the spiritual and only through France could we re-encounter our true spiritual past, which lay not in the barren plains of Castille, not in the heights of Machu Picchu, but in Greece, "the smile on the face of history." But if from Greece Rodó, a reader of *The Origin of Tragedy*, leads us to Nietzsche, well and good: the reading of Nietzsche gives *Ariel*, I think, its huskier moments; there is sometimes a lyrical-philosophical tone derived from *Zarathustra* and Rodó, on occasion, can rise to the excellent phrase, as in, "If we could cast the spirit of charity in the mold of Greek elegance, we would know perfection."

So be it: Rodó believes in a European ideality. America was, once, the Utopia of Renaissance Europe: Thomas More, Erasmus, Campanella, Montaigne, Shakespeare. In the nineteenth century, we turned Europe into our Utopia: Sarmiento, Lastarria, Rodó. Yet Rodó opposes the idea of imitation, quoting Michelet, who "believed that the mindless transferral of what is natural and spontaneous in one society to another where it has neither natural nor historical roots, was like attempting to introduce a dead organism into a living one by simple implantation."

Yes, we know all about the "extralogical imitation" described by the French sociologist Gabriel Tarde: goose-stepping South American armies, mansard roofs in Mexico City waiting for a tropical snowstorm, and glass boxes in São Paulo searching for a corner of consoling shade. I do not believe that is what Rodó the Europeanizer has in mind, since he does spell out what he wants: a cosmopolitanism which conciliates national identity and universal values of wholeness, since for Rodó cosmopolitanism "includes both fidelity to the past" and to "the formative forces" in Latin America. Rodó is welcoming a pluralistic totality, he is "seeing that Nature has more than one face, that humans have a variety of ideas and interests."

III

It is this idea, running, sometimes contradictorily, through *Ariel,* that sparks my interest in the book. It is an extremely important idea for our future: if, as I believe, Latin America has now achieved an identity, then it must pass the test of living with alternativity. You can cast this in political and economic terms, if you wish: we must pass from nationalism to interdependence, but interdependence is senseless without a basis in independence. Only independent nations can become interdependent partners. If not, they become protectorates, neocolonies, subject states.

On the cultural level, this means preserving your national or regional identity while testing it in the waters of alternativity. The Other defines our We. An isolated identity soon perishes; it can become folklore, mania, or specular theater. Worse: it will weaken and defeat us by lack of competition and points of comparison. The Greeks survived by meeting the Other: Persia or Rome, victorious or defeated. The Aztecs succumbed because they could not imagine their own alternative: the European world.

At the root of this problem is a way of living cultural values.

Both the Classics and the Romantics, for all their differences, shared faith in a culture made of organic values and striving toward unity, the value-in-itself which we mislaid along the way. Whether we lost it in Paradise, in Society, in Revolt, or through an Expense Account, *Unity* is what we must recover in order to be whole, classically or romantically.

The modern world makes this materially impossible. The last sigh of romantic yearning for unity was named the surrealists: Breton said it seriously, Buñuel with the wryest of ironies. Today, the rapid shifting and fragmentation of values, while it might make some yearn nostalgically for traditional, homogeneous, centripetal culture, is a fact. And, more than a fact, it is a value. It is a value for Bakhtin, for whom alternativity is a celebration, not a complaint, since the world needs my alternativity to give it meaning, and I need the difference of others to define myself: my identity can only be the "consciousness of the fact that I, in my most fundamental aspect of Myself, still am not."

It is a value for Theodor Adorno, who fears a forced reconciliation between subject and object (Man and Nature) and prefers the affirmation of difference and nonidentity in a freer, nonhierarchical world:. "A liberated mankind would by no means be a totality."

And certainly, for Max Weber, who baptized it: we are living a "polytheism" of values. Everything—communications, the economy, our sense of time and space, science, the new humanism—indicates that variety and not monotony, diversity and not unity, alternativity and not identity, the polytheism rather than the monotheism of values, shall define the coming century. There is an underlying felicity in all of this, and it is that it indicates that the values of the civil society, which are centrifugal, ungraspable, creative, will be seen as superior to the values of the centralized institutions, state, army, church, party, entrepreneurial dome, or whatever.

Now, in 1900, José Enrique Rodó chooses the discourse of only one of our options in Latin America. He is dismally uninterested in the many strands of Latin American culture. There is hardly a breath of Indian culture, Augustinian and Thomistic thought (politically so powerful in Latin America), or Renaissance Utopianism (a founding fact in Latin America). The baroque, Spanish mysticism, Spanish poetry and literature are absent from this discourse. It is, I repeat, the speech of an option: Latin America must be itself by being European, not through imitation, but through cosmopolitan absorption of the values of beauty, since beauty facilitates duty and goodness. This almost Scholastic conception of the Good and the Beautiful (one of the few times when Rodó lets his Thomistic skirt show) certainly informs the author's prose style. And it certainly provoked a tremendous reaction against such a style, which set the tone of our modern literature. The poetics of Neruda consisted in "walking around," seeing his ghost in windowpanes, making love in sweaty beds, gazing at his shoes, and eating artichokes. Vallejo cast a blind stone of anger and despair at Rodó's perfectly framed glass. Borges pared down his prose to the bare essentials. Gogol's "vulgar" or "poor" theme was in; Rodó's high-flown spirituality was out.

So, we come from a reaction to Rodó. But Rodó's rhetoric, his flowery spirituality, must be taken seriously because they perform the function of the thesis to which we can be antithetical. His is an honest thesis. His particular discourse, his intellectual option, is constantly aware that there is more; it is not pretentious in the sense of believing itself exclusive. If he claims the rights of the aristocratic against the democratic, he also admits that there will be no aristocracy that does not come, finally, from democracy itself, for an aristocracy based on hereditary privilege, cruel power, and irresponsibility is no aristocracy at all: it is not *the rule of the best*. This can only appear on the democratic scene; and the destruction of democratic values does not restore moral superiority or logical hierarchies. But if "we are all granted initial equality, subsequent inequality will be justified, since it will bear the sanction either of the mysterious selection of nature, or of meritorious effort of will. Considered in this way, democratic equality, far from conflicting with selection in customs and ideas, becomes the most efficient—in fact, the providential—instrument in spiritual selection." "Rationally conceived," adds Rodó, "democracy will always include an indispensable element of aristocracy," since a democracy, like an aristocracy, "will recognize the distinction of quality; but it will favor truly superior qualities—those of virtue, character and mind—and will not attempt to immobilize them in a class system that maintains the execrable privilege of caste."

Rodó's appetite for wholeness, inseparable from his honesty in admitting variety, is taken a step farther as he enters his debatable and chosen field: the spiritual versus the utilitarian. He opposes the value of contemplating the beautiful to the value of judging everything through the prism of immediate self-interest. He affirms that "a civilization acquires its character not from a display of prosperity, but from the grandeur of thought and feeling possible within it." But then he insists that historical proof favors a reciprocal relationship between the progress of the useful and the ideal. This dialectical compenetration he then applies not only to his critical praise of democracy (democracy must not be destroyed; it must be constantly reformed and bettered) but also to his highly relevant critique of the democracy of the United States of America.

IV

Rodó impressively enumerates the glories of the North American achievement: to have established "the grandeur and power of work" that antiquity had degraded to "the abjectness of slave labor"; to have identified work with human dignity, and to "have placed in the hands of the mechanic in his shop and the farmer in his field the mythic club of Hercules." The spirit of association, the summing up of individual strengths subordinated to research, philanthropy, and industry. Curiosity, the thirst for enlightenment, a reverence for public education. A prodigious skill for improvisation.

Rarely has such a glowing picture of North American virtues been offered, especially by a Latin American. The deficiencies of Rodó's judgment and information I have already noted; he is not well versed in North American literature. But he is uncannily on the mark when he asks questions that seem wholly pertinent today, since they are now being asked, as they were not in 1900, by North Americans themselves: Does the vast flow of information at our disposal mean that we are wiser or, paradoxically, more and more ignorant? Can barriers against vulgarity be created without damaging equality? Does the pursuit of well-being assure that we will have a destiny? And does energy—the prodigious, marvelous energy that is the supreme characteristic of the *gringos*—consume itself in movement and force without achieving the "legitimate demands of intellectual and moral dignity"?

Rodó says that he admires the United States, but does not love it. Those of us who both admire and love it can support and strengthen his critique and reaffirm his warning: "That powerful federation is effecting a kind of moral conquest among us. Admiration for its greatness and power is making impressive inroads in the minds of our leaders and, perhaps even more, in the impressionable minds of the masses, who are awed by its incontrovertible victories. And from admiring to imitating is an easy step."

The Uruguayan essayist's stance can be shared by many contemporaries, Latin and North Americans, who are currently worried about the overextension of North American power without the proper cultural, political, or even economic underpinnings to sustain it. Will the superpowers be powerful only because they are heavily armed? That is, I believe, a pitiful form of weakness. Deprive the USSR of arms: it doesn't cut much of a figure as a cultural or economic superpower. And the same, in a lesser degree, can be said of the United States. Rodó, unwittingly, announces an era of political and cultural diversification, best explained by the Spanish philosopher José Ortega y Gasset when in his *Theory of Andalucía* he writes that "life is first of all an ensemble of problems to which we answer with an ensemble of solutions called culture," but, "since many solutions are possible," it follows that a plurality of cultures have existed and shall exist. "What has never existed," concludes Ortega y Gasset, "is an absolute culture, that is, a culture responding successfully to every objection."

We have learned during our cruel century that, since there is no absolute culture, there can be no absolute politics. What exists are many cultures—many truths—expressing themselves through many kinds of politics. This is something that Rodó seemed to realize promptly, since he writes in 1900 what everyone, except the hard core of North American chauvinists, now clearly sees: "It would be futile to attempt to convince a North American that, although the contribution his nation has made to the evolution of liberty and utility has undoubtedly been substantial, and should rightly qualify as a universal contribution, indeed, as a contribution to *humanity*, it is not so great as to cause the axis of the world to shift in the direction of a new Capitol."

Rodó could be speaking of a few crazy bureaucrats, power-hungry preachers and other assorted plastic Messiahs when he says that certain North Americans, "given the opportunity," would gladly revise *Genesis: In the beginning, there was the USA*. I do not know if Rodó is right when he says that nature has given North Americans neither the genius for persuasion nor the vocation of the apostle. As a matter of fact, I think he is wrong on this point. We have recently seen a parade of zealots out to achieve what Rodó, ambiguously, sees as the possibility (or impossibility) of American hegemony. No, such hegemony is each day lessened because the world, not by being anti-American, but simply by being itself, more and more frequently denies the United States the privilege of hegemony. Rodó's 1900 warnings are eerily echoed by a contemporary Hungarian writer, an articulate speaker for his nation's freedom and opponent of Soviet suzerainty, the novelist George Konrad: The United States, he writes from Budapest in 1987, as Rodó wrote from Montevideo in 1900, should cease to be obsessed by its lecture-platform self-congratulations as the strongest, the richest, the freest, the noblest, the most unselfish of nations, over-reacting neurotically to every setback and every challenge, seeing intrigue, ingratitude, and Communist machinations wherever other people, having interests that do not coincide with those of the United States, insist on pursuing them anyway.

This mighty paranoia can be accompanied by a growing sense of schizophrenia. *Democracy or empire?* Leonard Barnes asked of Great Britain in 1939, in his study of the colonial question.

Britain solved its problems of empire by having a late and weak state at home, where a strong aristocracy represented a part of the society and an emerging middle class wrested power from it, while the foreign enterprises had a commercial more than an ideological ring to them—Kipling notwithstanding.

[24]

But Britain, ideologically, never promised to take democracy anywhere. Its crusade was for mercantile gain, political influence, security, nonmingling of races, and the fetish of "progress," "the white man's burden." Britain called itself an empire and accepted its actions as imperialistic.

Britain was far too ironical to confuse its internal democratic developments with its external actions in the realm of *realpolitik*. Needless to say, the Soviet Union has even less of a dualism: it has acted as an empire internally and externally, with no fissures.

The United States has cast itself in the role of democracy inside and out. But a mixture of ignorance, necessity, and blindness has aligned it with some of the most undemocratic regimes of the postwar period, from Somoza in Nicaragua to the shah in Iran.

When these individuals are overthrown, the United States has not had sufficient flexibility to normalize relations with their successors, even when they—Sandinistas or ayotollahs— have been simply working their understandable anti-American fevers out of their bodies. The United States either becomes supportive of the counter-revolutionaries, compounding its original Somocista sins by being perceived as the enemy of Nicaraguan autonomy and the manipulator of rebels totally armed by, directed by, and servile to the USA, or it seeks the strangest avenues—signed Bibles, chocolate cakes, disreputable arms salesmen, inanely provincial NSC strategists, gung-ho comic strip Rambos—to go beyond the realities it dislikes. In both cases, the USA falls prey to the small enemy it has aggrandized, is left without options, and opens itself up to tearing internal debates. Why does the United States exhibit such a disparity between the way it acts internally (democratically) and the way it acts externally (through deception, intervention, violation of international law, and, if need be, violent military actions against weaker nations)?

The extreme danger of this situation is that the USA will decide, like the USSR, to unify its internal and external imperial policies. But this would mean the end of democracy in the United States—or, more likely, an internal conflict of revolutionary dimensions to decide the issue. But it could also mean a unity of internal and external democratic policy. The United States would then quickly outstrip the Soviet Union in support around the world. Its popularity would be its greatest strength. But it should not confuse democratic conduct with the imposition of US-style democracy abroad. It should correctly identify it with respect for the workings of politics in foreign contexts totally alien, at times, to US values. Normal relations, constructive and cooperative, with all, independent of anyone's internal politics and ideologies. This is the demand that the hyperactive, self-congratulating, and provincial part of the United States cannot countenance.

Few comparisons, then, are as useful for a North American understanding of the Other as comparison with the otherness of the countries that it shares this hemisphere with. We are the strangers that the United States must understand first of all. We are the Other at the doorstep, not in the backyard, but in a house with its own name, dimensions, design, style, and purposes: Latin America.

V

It is a pity that Rodó did not apply his critical thought to Latin America more than to the United States or to the glorification of the European and Classical ideals. *Ariel* would have been a different book—the book it had the potential to be—had the critique of the United States been accompanied by a comparable critique of Latin America and had Rodó developed the ensuing comparison. He would, perhaps, have arrived at similar conclusions: we are both, North and Latin Americans, still projects of history, incomplete societies, working models, not paradigms of perfection. Rodó barely brushes by the beginnings of a cultural critique of Latin America when he has, I might say, "the urban intuition": "In terms of conditions here in our America, the need to define the true concept of our social regimes becomes doubly imperative. Our democratic countries have grown very swiftly, swollen by the uninterrupted growth of our cities. Large numbers of immigrants have been added to a nucleus still too weak to assimilate and channel properly this flood of humanity in ways that can be provided by a solid secular social structure, a secure political system, and deeply rooted personal values. This situation conjures up the future danger of a democratic deterioration."

This uncanny forecast of the society, debt-ridden, inflation-haunted, politically brittle and socially incendiary, in which we are now living can be set against a comparable North American crisis. The crisis of the fledgling urban society in Latin America and the crisis of the melting-pot society in the USA. As parallel events, "the assimilative energy that has allowed them to preserve a certain uniformity and a certain generic character in spite of waves of ethnic groups very different from those that have until now set the tone for their national identity will be vitiated in increasingly difficult battles."

As the homogeneous civil society of the United States faces the immigration of the vastly heterogeneous and, what is even worse, of the proximate (Latin America), we (in Latin America) face the challenge of a heterogeneous civil society invading the formerly homogeneous spaces of political, military, and religious power. It is a fascinating thing to contemplate; it implies that the destiny of our respective civil societies is far more important than the duels between our national states, and it makes us wonder at, appreciate, and deplore both the quality of Rodó's intuition and his inability to develop it more thoroughly. It is not a question of hindsight. Rodó had enough social, cultural, and historical elements surrounding him in Latin America to do so.

Irritating, insufferable, admirable, stimulating, disappointing Rodó: our Uruguayan uncle, sitting in a corner of our family portrait, letting us become ourselves as we push him into the shadows, then realize that he has something to say yet: we give you the limelight again and then, old man, we bang you over the head again. So, you are part of our family quarrels and must bear with your disrespectful, equally disappointed, intuitive, incomplete nephews, living in a world that you helped define for us, and offered unto our revolt.

CARLOS FUENTES
Cambridge University, England
Spring 1987

ARIEL

To the youth of America.

*T*hat afternoon, at the end of a year of classes, the venerable old teacher, who by allusion to the wise magician of Shakespeare's *Tempest* was often called Prospero, was bidding his young disciples farewell, gathering them about him one last time.

The students were already present in the large classroom in which an exquisite yet austere decor honored in every fastidious detail the presence of Prospero's books, his faithful companions. An exquisite bronze of *The Tempest*'s Ariel, like the presiding spirit of that serene atmosphere, dominated the room. It was the teacher's custom to sit beside this statue, and this is why he had come to be called Prospero, the magician who in the play is attended and served by the fanciful figure depicted by the sculptor. Perhaps, however, an even deeper reason and meaning for the name lay in the master's teaching and character.

Shakespeare's ethereal Ariel symbolizes the noble, soaring aspect of the human spirit. He represents the superiority of reason and feeling over the base impulses of irrationality. He is generous enthusiasm, elevated and unselfish motivation in all actions, spirituality in culture, vivacity and grace in intelligence. Ariel is the ideal toward which human selection ascends, the force that wields life's eternal chisel, effacing from aspiring mankind the clinging vestiges of Caliban, the play's symbol of brutal sensuality.

The regal statue represented the "airy spirit" at the very moment when Prospero's magic sets him free, the instant he is about to take wing and vanish in a flash of light. Wings unfolded; gossamer, floating robes damascened by the caress of sunlight on bronze; wide brow uplifted; lips half-parted in a serene smile—everything in Ariel's pose perfectly anticipated the graceful beginnings of flight. Happily, the inspired artist who formed his image in solid sculpture had also preserved his angelic appearance and ideal airiness.

Deep in thought, Prospero stroked the statue's brow. Then he seated the young men about him and in a firm voice—a *masterful* voice capable of seizing an idea and implanting it deep within the listener's mind with all the penetrating illumination of a beam of light, the incisive ring of chisel on marble, or the life-infusing touch of brush upon canvas or sculpting wave upon sand—he began to speak, surrounded by his affectionate and attentive students.

*H*ere beside the statue that has daily witnessed our friendly gatherings—from which I have tried to remove any unwelcome austerity—I am going to speak with you one last time, so that our farewell may be the seal stamped on a covenant of emotions and ideas.

I call upon Ariel to be my numen, so that my words will be the most subtle and most persuasive I have ever spoken. I believe that to address the young on any noble and elevated subject is a kind of sacred discourse. I also believe that a young mind is hospitable soil in which the seed of a single timely word will quickly yield immortal fruit.

It is my wish to collaborate on but one page of the agenda that you will draw up in your innermost being and shape with your personal moral character and strength while preparing to breathe the free air of action. This individual agenda—which sometimes may be formulated or written but sometimes is revealed only during the course of action itself—is always to be found in the spirit of those groups and peoples who rise above the multitudes. If, when referring to the philosophy of individual choice, Goethe could say with such profundity that the only man worthy of liberty and life is the man capable of winning them for himself with each new day, can it not also be said—with even greater truth—that the honor of each generation requires it to win liberty and life through its increasing intellectual activity, its own particular efforts, its faith in resolutely expressing the ideal, and its place in the evolution of ideas?

As you earn yours, you must begin by recognizing in yourselves a first article of faith. The youth you are now living is a form of power; it is you who must employ it. And it is a treasure: it is you who must invest it. Cherish that treasure, that power; never lose your burning pride in it, and use it well. I agree with Ernest Renan: "Youth is the discovery of a boundless horizon: Life." This discovery of unexplored worlds must then be completed with the manly strength that conquers them. And no spectacle can be imagined that is more likely to excite both the interest of the thinker and the inspiration of the artist than that of a generation marching toward its future, eager for action, heads high, smiles revealing a haughty disdain for the possibility of disillusion, hearts inspired by visions of bountiful and remote lands, like the Cipango and El Dorado of the heroic chronicles of the Conquistadors.

From the rebirth of human hopes, from the eternal promise that the future will bring the realization of all that is good, the soul awakening to life acquires its beauty—an ineffable beauty composed, like the dawn in Victor Hugo's *Contemplations,* of a "vestige of dream and beginning of thought."

The fact that in generation after generation, humanity can, in spite of the harsh experiences of centuries, renew its undying hope and its eager faith in an ideal, recalled to Jean-Marie

Guyau the obsession of the poor deranged woman whose strange and moving madness was to believe, every day, that this was the day she was to be married. The plaything of her hallucination, each morning she placed upon her pale brow the bridal coronet with its filmy veil. With a sweet smile she prepared to receive her illusory groom, until at nightfall her hours of waiting brought the inevitable disillusion, and her madness became tinged with melancholy. But with the dawn her naïve faith returned; innocent of past disenchantment and murmuring, "Today he will come," she again put on the coronet and veil, again smiled, and again happily awaited her beloved.

In the same way, no sooner does an ideal die than humanity puts on its gala nuptial attire and awaits the dreamed ideal with the same renewed faith, the same tenacious and touching madness. Awakening that renewal—as regular as the seasons—has in all ages been the responsibility of the young: the bridal headdress is woven from the spirits of each human spring. Pessimism may attempt to suppress the sublime stubbornness of hope that bursts forth from dejection, but in vain. Whether based in reason or born of experience, no pessimism can oppose the proud call "Onward!" that wells from the essence of Life. There are times when, apparently because of some missed beat in the triumphal rhythm, generations that from birth are destined to personify vacillation and weakness pass through history. But pass they do; not, perhaps, without having had their ideas like any other generation—even if negative and unfeeling. Then once again in humankind shines the hope for the long-awaited Husband whose sweet and radiant image, as in the pristine verses of the mystics, is sufficient reason for living, for happiness, even though it is never to appear in the flesh.

In contrast, youth—which symbolizes light and love and energy, for individuals, for generations, and also for the evolutionary process of society—does exist. Fruitfulness, strength, dominion over the future, will always belong to peoples who feel about life as you do. There was an era when the attributes of youth were, more than in any other age, the attributes of a people, the character of a civilization, a time when a breath of captivating adolescence left its trace on the serene brow of an entire race. When Greece was born, the gods granted it the secret of their eternal youth. Greece is the soul of youth. "He who in Delphi contemplates the swarming throngs of Ionians," says a Homeric hymn, "cannot imagine they will ever grow old." Greece accomplished greatness because it possessed the youthful attributes of the joy that is the source of action and the enthusiasm that is the all-powerful lever. The Egyptian priest, with whom Solon spoke in the temple of Saïs, said to that Athenian legislator, pitying the Greeks for their noisy garrulousness: "You are no more than children!" And Jules Michelet compared the activities of the Greeks to a festive game around which all the nations of the world gathered and smiled. But from these divine "children's" games on the shores of the Archipelago and beneath the shadow of the Ionian olive trees were born art, philosophy, free thought, scientific curiosity, and awareness of human dignity—all the God-given stimuli that still serve as our inspiration and our pride. Meanwhile, absorbed in its hierarchic austerity, Egypt, the land of the priest, represented a senescence that focused its teachings on eternal repose and dismissed all frivolity with a disdainful hand. Grace and action were barred from its spiritual attitudes, as was life from its icons. Now when posterity turns its eyes to that land, all it sees is a sterile order presiding over the evolution of a civilization that existed only to weave its shroud and build its sepulchres: the shadow of the architect's compass stretching across the sterility of the sands.

Enthusiasm and hope—the signs of the youthful spirit—correspond in the harmonics of history and nature to movement and light. Wherever you turn your eyes, you will find that those gifts are the natural environment for all things beautiful and strong. Then lift your eyes to the highest example of all. The Christian idea—upon which still weighs the accusation of having cast a shadow over the world by proscribing the gaiety of paganism—is essentially of youthful inspiration, as long as it does not wander far from its origins. Newborn Christianity, in Renan's interpretation—one I find all the more accurate for its poetry—is a portrait of youth that can never fade. The heavenly perfume that floated above the leisurely passage of the Master through the fields of Galilee was composed of youth or, which is the same, of living dream, grace, and candor. This aroma permeated the sermons He delivered, with no trace of repentant gravity, beside a sky-blue lake and in fruitful valleys, witnessed by the "fowls of the air" and the "lilies of the field" that enrich the parables, as He painted the joy of the "Kingdom of God" upon the sweet smile of Nature. The ascetics who accompanied John the Baptist during his penance in the wilderness are missing from this blissful picture. When Jesus speaks of those who follow Him, He compares them to the groom's attendants in a wedding procession. It is the impression of divine contentment—joined with the essence of the new faith—that we sense throughout the odyssey of the Evangelists. This is the contentment that spreads its innocent happiness, its ingenuous *joie de vivre,* through the first Christian communities. And this the contentment that as it reaches Rome and the unknown and unknowing Christians of Transtevere finds an easy path into their hearts, triumphing by counterposing the enchantment of their inner youth—the youth of souls perfumed by the libation of the new wine—to the severity of the stoics and the decadence of the worldly.

So, then, you must be fully aware of that sacred strength you carry within you. Realize, however, that in the material world it can go astray and die of inertia like a spent projectile. That precious treasure is the gift of nature, but its generative force lies in ideas, and should it be wasted or dispersed in individual consciousness, it will not benefit mankind. In the pages of an excellent novel—that genre whose vast mirrored surface has reflected life in the last dizzying hundred years—a learned author of our century described the psychology of youth as seen in the generations between Chateaubriand's Réné and Huysmans' Des Esseintes. His analysis established a progressive diminution of *inner youthfulness* and energy through a series of representative characters beginning with the sick, but often virile and passionately intense, heroes of the Romantics, and ending with such enervated, spiritless persons as the protagonist of Huysmans' *A rebours* or Robert Greslous in Paul Bourget's *Le disciple,* who reflect the depressing manifestations of the spirit of our time. But his analysis also proved a heartening rebirth of spirit and hope in the psychology of youth, which we find in a literature that may presage more profound changes: a rebirth personified in the new heroes of Jules Lemaître, Téodor de Wyzewa, and Edouard Rod, and whose most perfect representation is perhaps to be found in David Grieve, a character from Mrs. Humphrey Ward's *The History of David Grieve*. In Grieve, this contemporary English novelist brought together in a single character all the pain and all the restless ideas of several generations, then resolved them in a supreme dénouement of serenity and love.

Will this hope be fulfilled? You who, like the journeyman to his workplace, are marching toward the gateway to the twentieth century, will you leave in the art that depicts *you* images more triumphant than those left by my century? If the divine era when youth was the model for the brilliant dialogues of Plato was possible only in the brief springtime of our world, if we are constrained "not to consider the gods," as Phorkyas in Faust counsels the chorus of captives, should we not at least be allowed to dream? May we not hope for the emergence of generations that would restore idealism and active enthusiasm to life? Generations in which sentiment would be a powerful force? Generations in which a vigorous rebirth of will would put to flight the moral cowardice nourished in the breast of dejection and doubt? Can youth again be an essential element in society, as it is in individual life?

This is my cause for concern as I face you today. Your first pages, the revelations of your innermost world, speak of indecision, often of amazement, although never of enervation or loss of will. I know that enthusiasm pulses strongly within you. I also know that the discouragement and sorrow that sincere thought—a virtue greater even than hope—dredged from the depths of your meditation and from the inevitable doubts you encountered there, are not an indication of a permanent state of mind. Nor do they signify any lack of confidence in the eternal potential of Life. Anytime a cry of anguish has risen from the depths of your hearts, you have not stifled it with the mute pride of the tortured Stoic, but transformed it with a note of messianic hope into an invocation to the ideal *that is to come.*

I must make clear, however, that when I speak to you of enthusiasm and hope, of lofty, creative virtues, I do not mean that you should erect a barrier between skepticism and faith, or between dejection and joy. Nothing is farther from my mind than the idea of confusing the natural attributes of youth and their lively spontaneity with a frivolous manner of thinking that, because it conceives of action as nothing more than an excuse for play, buys contentment at the price of rejecting what is mysterious and serious in life. That is not the nobility of an individual's youth, nor of the youth of a people. I have always disagreed with those who appointed themselves as watchdogs over the destiny of America and as custodians of its tranquillity zealously attempted to stifle, even before it reaches us, any resonance of human sorrow, any echo of foreign literatures, whose pessimism or degeneracy might endanger the fragility of their optimism. No enlightened intelligence can be based in naïve isolation or voluntary ignorance. Every problem that doubt can pose to the human intellect, every sincere rebuke hurled from the breast of dejection and sorrow against God or Nature, deserves our conscious consideration. We must prove our strength of heart by accepting the challenge of the Sphinx, not by avoiding its formidable questions. Remember, too, that the beginnings of action, of fruitful ideas, lodge in bitter as well as in joyous thought. When sorrow is debilitating, when sorrow leads irresistibly to stagnation, or when it treacherously counsels inaction, then the philosophy at its heart is unworthy of youthful souls. Then indeed may a José Joaquín Olmedo, as in "En la muerte de Da María de Borbón," call it an "indolent soldier that militates beneath the banners of death." But when what emerges from sorrow is the desire to struggle to recover the well-being that has been denied us, then sorrow acts as a goad to evolution, as life's most powerful motivating force. This is why Helvetius believed that by causing our sensibility to prevent our slipping into idleness, and thus becoming an incentive for action, ennui could become the most precious of all human prerogatives.

In this sense, it has been wisely stated that pessimism is a kind of *paradoxical optimism*. Far from postulating the renunciation and condemnation of life, such pessimism, in its dissatisfaction with present reality, prompts change. What humanity must protect, against all pessimistic negation, is not so much the idea of the relative good of the present as that of the possibility of arriving at a better condition through a progress hastened and directed by human beings. Faith in the future and confidence in the efficacy of human strength are the necessary antecedents for all energetic actions and all productive plans. That is why this afternoon I have chosen to begin by recommending to you the undying excellence of the faith that, because it is instinctual, youth need not be taught. You will find it simply by allowing Nature's divine suggestion to work within you.

[39]

Animated by faith, go forth into life, now opening its broad horizons before you. Go with the noble ambition to make your presence felt from the moment you confront life's challenge with the proud gaze of a conqueror. Audacious initiative and innovative brilliance permeate the youthful spirit. Perhaps today, across the world, the action and influence of youth are on the march in societies less effective and intense than they should have been. Gaston Deschamps recently pointed this out in France, commenting on the late initiation of youthful generations into the public life and culture of that nation and the limited originality with which they had contributed to forming its predominant ideas. Insofar as we may speak in generalities, given the painful isolation in which we Latin peoples live, my impression of the present time in our America perhaps justifies a similar observation. Nevertheless, I believe that I see everywhere the need for a revitalization, for a revelation of new strengths. I believe that America is in great need of her youth. This is why I am addressing myself to you. This is why I am so extraordinarily interested in your moral orientation. The energy of your word and your example can combine the living strength of the past with the work of the future. Like Michelet, I believe that the true concept of education not only embraces the acculturation of the sons through the experience of their fathers, but also, and frequently even more importantly, that of the fathers through the innovative inspiration of their sons.

Let us speak, then, of how to assess the life that lies before you.

he many vocations available to you will dictate that you travel in diverse directions and will determine a different temperament and distinctive aptitude in each of you. Some among you will be men of science, others artists, still others men of action. The profound awareness of the fundamental unity of our natures, however, must take precedence over the predilections that bind each of us to our different ways of life. This unity demands that the primary aim of each individual should be to live an unblemished and exemplary life in which nobility and selflessness are communicated before any other faculty. More compelling than professional and cultural variation is our individual responsibility to contribute to the common destiny of rational beings. "There is one profession, which is that of being *man*," was Guyau's profound observation. And Renan, in his assessment of unequal and undeveloped civilizations, reminds us that the goal of man cannot be exclusively to learn, or feel, or imagine, but, rather, to be truly and wholly *human*. This is the ideal of perfection toward which each of us must channel his energies, with the hope that as one individual he may represent the species in miniature.

Aspire, then, to develop to the fullest possible measure the totality of your being—not merely one aspect of it. Do not shrug your shoulders before any noble or creative manifestation of human nature under the pretext that your individuality and preferences bind you to a different one. When you cannot be a participant, you can be an attentive spectator. There is a certain false and vulgarized concept that conceives of education as totally subordinate to a utilitarian end. Such utilitarianism, with its attendant premature specialization, mutilates spiritual integrity and tends to suppress from learning all that is selfless and ideal. This process does not sufficiently take into account the danger of preparing for the future narrow minds that because they can see no reality other than the most immediate will live in icy isolation, separated from others in the same society who have chosen different ways of life.

The fact that each of us must dedicate himself to a specific activity, to a single mode in our culture, does not in any way prevent our hearing the symphony of the spirit and realizing the common destiny of all rational beings. That single activity, that specific cultural mode, will be but one basic note in the harmony of the whole. The famous assertion by the slave of antiquity, "I am a man, nothing human is alien to me," is an eternal truth that will resonate forever in our consciousness. Our capacity to understand must be limited only by our inability to comprehend narrow minds. To be incapable of seeing that Nature has more than one face, that humans have a variety of ideas and interests, is to live in a shadowy dreamworld penetrated by a single ray of light. When intolerance and exclusivity are born of the tyranny that can be imposed by inspiration, or of the obsessiveness that can result from even the most ideal and selfless project, they may be justified—even deserving of sympathy. When, however, intolerance arises from vulgarity, when it attests the limitations of a mind incapable of reflecting more than a partial appearance of things, then intolerance becomes the most abominable of inferiorities.

Unhappily, it is in civilizations that have achieved a whole and refined culture that the danger of spiritual limitation is most real and leads to the most dreaded consequences. In fact, to the degree that culture advances, the law of evolution, manifesting itself in society as in nature to be a growing tendency toward heterogeneity, seems to require a corresponding limitation in individual aptitudes and the inclination to restrict more severely each individual's field of action. While it is a necessary condition to progress, the development of specialization brings with it visible disadvantages, which are not limited to narrowing the horizon of individual intelligences and which inevitably falsify our concept of the world. Specialization, because of the great diversity of individual preferences and habits, is also damaging to a sense of solidarity. Auguste Comte has tellingly noted this danger in advanced civilizations. In his view, the most serious flaw in a state of high social perfection lies in the frequency with which it produces deformed spirits, spirits extremely adept in one aspect of life but monstrously inept in all others. The manner in which the mind is diminished by continual commerce within a single category of ideas or by the exercise of a single mode of activity is, for Comte, comparable to the miserable fate of the worker who is obliged by the division of labor in his workplace to consume his life's energies in the unvarying routine of one mechanical chore. In both cases, the result is a disastrous indifference to the general interests of humankind. And although—happily, the French Positivist adds—this kind of human automation represents the extreme of the disjunctive influence of specialization, the reality—already frequently observable—demands that we weigh his comments very seriously.

This disjunction of which I have spoken is as damaging to the *aesthetic* of the social structure as it is to its solidarity. The incomparable beauty of Athens, the longevity of the model this goddess of a city bequeathed to us, were owing to a concept of life based on the total harmony of all human faculties and the mutual agreement that all energies should be directed toward the glory and power of mankind. Athens knew how to exalt both the ideal and the real, reason and instinct, the forces of the spirit and those of the body. It sculpted all four faces of the soul. Every free Athenian drew around himself a perfect circle to contain his actions, and no disturbing impulse was allowed to impinge upon the graceful proportions within that sphere. The Greek was an athlete and an animated sculpture in the Gymnasium; a citizen on the Pnyx; a debater and intellectual in the Forum. He exercised his will in a broad range of activities, and his intellect in many creative endeavors. This is why Macaulay argued that one day of public life in Attica offered a more brilliant program of instruction than any we draw up in our modern institutions. And from that free and unique flowering of fully developed human nature was born the *Greek miracle*— an inimitable blend of activity and serenity: the spring of the human spirit; a sparkling moment in history.

In our times, the increasing complexity of our civilization would seem to preclude any serious thought of recapturing the harmony possible only in an age of grace and simplicity. But within the complexity of our culture, within the progressive diversity of characters, skills, and values that is the inescapable consequence of progress, it is still reasonable to hope that all human beings may be aware of the fundamental ideas and sentiments that ensure the harmony of life—the *spiritual concerns* to which no rational human being may remain indifferent.

When a sense of materialism and comfort dominates a society as energetically as it does today, the effects of the narrow mind and the single-faceted culture are particularly calamitous for the diffusion of ideals. Although venerated by those who denote their noblest energy to it, for the vast majority of others the ideal remains a remote and perhaps not-even-suspected area of life. All manner of selfless meditation, ideal contemplation, and individual tranquillity in which the daily struggle of the utilitarian yields briefly to the serenity that comes from the more elevated gaze of reason are in contemporary society unknown to millions of otherwise civilized and cultivated individuals whose education or habits reduce them to the automatism of strictly materialistic activities. Yes, this kind of servitude must be the most dismal and opprobrious of all moral damnations. I exhort you to defend yourselves, to be militant in preventing your spirit from being mutilated by the tyranny of a single, or a self-interested, objective. Never devote more than a part of yourselves to utility, or to passion. Even within material servitude, the inner self, the self of reason and sentiment, may remain free. Do not, then, use the excuse of commitment to work or responsibilities to justify the enslavement of your spirit.

What now comes to my mind from a dusty corner of memory is a story that illustrates what our souls should be. There was once a patriarchal King who lived in the fabled and uncomplicated Oriental lands that served as the happy source of so many tales. This King reigned during the innocent years of the tents of Ishmael and the palaces of Pylos. In man's memory he came to be called the Hospitable King. The charity of this King was inexhaustible. Any misfortune seemed to disappear in the boundlessness of his mercy as if sinking of its own weight. The hungry seeking bread were drawn to his generous welcome, as were the sick at heart longing for the balm of a soothing word. Like the most sensitive sounding board, this King's heart resonated to the rhythms of those about him. His palace was the home of all his people. Freedom and liveliness reigned within this majestic edifice, and no guards stood at the gates to deny entry. Among the open colonnades, shepherds at their leisure played their rustic serenades; old men gathered to gossip as evening fell; and serene groups of young women arranged blossoms and boughs in willow baskets—the only taxes exacted in the kingdom. Merchants from Ophir, traders from Damascus, came and went through the wide gates at all hours, and a wealth of silks, jewels, and perfumes competed for the King's attention. The weary pilgrim found his rest beside the King's very throne. Birds flocked at midday to peck crumbs from his table, and at dawn rollicking bands of children ran to the foot of the bed where the silver-bearded King slept, to announce the new day. The King's infinite generosity extended to both the hapless and the inanimate. Nature, too, felt the attraction of the King's generosity. As in the myth of Orpheus and the legend of St. Francis of Assisi, winds, birds, plants seemed to befriend human creatures in that oasis of hospitality. From the seed that fell into the cracks of paving stones and walls sprang lilies to beautify the ruins, with no cruel hands to pluck them or evil foot to crush them. Bold and curious vines twined through the wide-flung windows of the King's own chambers. Exhausted winds wafted their cargo of aromas and harmonies into the royal castle. Waves from the nearby sea sprayed its walls with their foam, as if wishing to enfold the castle in their embrace. And an edenic freedom, a vast aura of mutual trust, created an ambience of eternal celebration . . .

But deep within, very deep within, isolated from the hubbub of the castle by covered passageways hidden from the view of the unrefined—like Ludwig Uhland's "lost chapel" in the far reaches of the forest—at the end of secret paths lay a mysterious room that no one except the King himself was permitted to enter. As he crossed that threshold, his hospitality changed to ascetic egoism. Thick bulwarks enclosed the room. Not an echo from the boisterous world outside, not a note from nature's symphony, not a word from human lips, penetrated the carved porphyry that lined the walls or stirred the air in the forbidden retreat. A worshipful silence reigned in the still, unsullied air. The light, filtered through stained glass, descended quietly, majestically, into the hall, then amid celestial calm, melted like a snowflake fallen in a warm nest. Never was there such peace—not in the ocean grotto, not in the sylvan solitude. Sometimes, when the night was diaphanous and tranquil, the ornately medallioned ceiling parted like the two halves of a shell, allowing magnificent shadows to seep into the mother-of-pearl. Chaste waves of nenuphar wafted through the room, the perfume that suggests drowsy contemplation and profound soul-searching. Somber caryatids guarded the marble entries, admonishing all to silence. The carved images of the canopy above the bed whispered of idealism, contemplation, repose.

. . . And even though no human accompanied the aged King to his mysterious refuge, his hospitality was as generous as ever—but now the guests gathered within his walls were impalpable and insubstantial. In this room, the legendary King dreamed; in it he escaped reality; in it his meditations turned inward and his thoughts were polished like pebbles by the tide. In this sanctum sanctorum Psyche unfolded her snowy wings upon his brow. . . . And then, when death came to remind the King that he was but a guest in his own palace, the impregnable chamber sank into eternal quiet, eternal repose. No one ever profaned it by entering irreverently where the aged King had wished to be alone in the Ultima Thule of his soul.

Your inner life is like this parable. Like the palace of the trusting King, it opens, with salutary generosity, to all the world. At the same time, it contains a hidden and mysterious cell where no profane guest, only serene reason, may enter. Not until you enter that inviolable stronghold may you truly call yourselves free men. Those men are not free who lose dominion of self by yielding to unruly passion or utilitarian interests. They forget that, according to Montaigne's wise precept, we may lend our spirit, but not forfeit it. Thought, dream, appreciation: these are the subtle visitors to my cell. The ancients, in their wisdom, included my visitors within the family of *otium*, the wise use of leisure, which they held as the highest example of rational life—thought freed from any ignoble yoke. Noble leisure was the investment of time that they expressed as a superior mode of life opposed to commercial enterprise. Having linked the concept of dignity of life exclusively with the aristocratic idea of repose, the spirit of classicism finds its correction and its complement in our modern belief in the dignity of labor. The rhythm formed from repose and action is so desirable that no man should need urging to maintain it. The Stoics, whose philosophy illuminated the decline of antiquity like a shining precursor of Christianity, bequeathed to us in the beautiful figure of Cleanthes a simple and moving image of the salvation of the inner freedom that may survive even in servitude. This slave, forced to expend his great strength in drawing water to fill the pails that turned a millstone, gave himself over to meditation in the brief interludes from his strenuous labors, and with his calloused hand traced on the cobblestones the maxims he had heard from the lips of Zeno. All rational education, all perfection of our natures, should begin by simulating the two modes symbolized in Cleanthes.

Again I say to you: your basic principle, your motto in life, must be to maintain the integrity of the human condition. Nothing should ever take precedence over this supreme goal. No single enterprise can satisfy the rational goals of individual existence or produce harmony in collective existence. Thus, in the same way that exclusivity of action or culture deforms individuals, glory is ephemeral in societies that have stifled the free development of sensibility and thought, either with mercantilism, as in Phoenicia; or war, as in Sparta; or mysticism, as during the terror of millenarianism; or the salon, as in eighteenth-century France. And so as you guard against the mutilation of your morality, and while aspiring to the harmonious growth and nobility of your being, remember also that the most frequent of contemporary mutilations is one that forces the soul to deprive itself of the *inner life* that is the natural ambience of everything delicate and noble, the inner life that when exposed to harsh reality will be scorched by the breath of impure passion and stunted by the self-interest of utilitarianism. Selfless meditation, ideal contemplation, the *otium* of ancient times, and the impregnable chamber of my tale are necessary components of this inner life.

ecause the first act of profanation will be directed against the most sacred area of the sanctuary, the kind of debasing regression I now caution you against will begin with rejection of all that is delicate. Of all the desirable elements of a rational existence, the sense of the beautiful, the clear vision of the beauty of things, is the sense most quickly withered by the sterile and repetitious daily round, making of it an attribute to be preserved by a minority in that society as an abandoned treasure. A feeling for beauty is to the sense of the ideal as enamel to the ring. With rough treatment it begins to wear away and is inevitably effaced. In this way, absolute indifference comes to take the place of universal love. The stupefaction of the savage, when confronted with the tools and products of civilization, is no greater than the amazement of a relatively larger number of cultivated men when they witness behavior that gives serious weight to what is beautiful in life.

Judas' argument that Mary uselessly annointed Jesus' feet with a pound of ointment of spikenard still stands as a formula of frugality. A superfluity of art is not worth the three hundred pence to the anonymous masses. If they *do* respect art, it is only as an esoteric cult. Nonetheless, of all the elements of education that ennoble life, none is more worthy of universal interest than art, because as Schiller has ably illustrated, nothing is more conducive to a culture that is *broad* and complete, in the sense of stimulating all the soul's faculties.

Even if love and appreciation of beauty did not respond to some essential need in rational man, or if they were not in themselves deserving of cultivation, a higher morality would dictate a culture of aesthetics simply in the best interests of society. No one is averse to educating the moral sensibility, and preparing the individual to appreciate beauty should be implicit in that education. Never forget that an educated sense of the beautiful is the most effective collaborator in the formation of a delicate sensitivity for justice. Dignity and inner nobility will find no greater artisan. Never will an individual be more faithful to duty than when he moves from believing that beauty is something that originates outside himself to feeling it internally as aesthetic harmony. And never will that individual know goodness more fully than when he learns to respect the sense of beauty in others.

It is true that the sanctity of good works can purify and elevate grossness. Good may be done without the external appearance of beauty. Charity may achieve sublime effects through vulgar, distasteful, and coarse means. But charity given with delicacy and good taste is not only more beautiful, it is finer, because it adds a further benefit to the gift: a gentle and unique caress that with its warm glow enhances the benefice bestowed.

To communicate beauty is a work of mercy. I have always believed that he who demands that good and truth be expressed with sternness and severity is a treacherous friend to good and truth. Virtue is also a form of art—a divine art: she smiles upon her daughters, the Graces. Teaching that attempts to instill in our spirits the idea of duty, as well as the idea of gravity, must conceive of those ideas as the highest poetry. Guyau, king of elegant analogies, suggested a correspondence that is perfect for illustrating the dual objective of moral culture. He evokes the finely sculpted choir of a Gothic cathedral, where carving inspired by deep faith reveals on one surface the scenes of a saint's life and, on the other, ornamental garlands. Thus for every scene depicting the saint's piety or his martyrdom, for every feature and every attitude, there was on the reverse side a corolla or petal. For example, as the symbolic representation of good, a lily bloomed, or a rose. Guyau believes that our soul is undoubtedly sculpted in the same manner. And is not he himself, an apostle of evangelical beauty, an example of such harmony?

There is no doubt in my mind that one who has learned to distinguish the delicate from the vulgar, the ugly from the beautiful, has made half the journey toward distinguishing good from evil. This is not to say that good taste, as a certain moral dilettantism would have it, is the only criterion for appreciating the legitimacy of human actions. But neither, using the criterion of strict asceticism, should good taste be considered a snare and a delusion. I do not suggest that taste is the most direct path to good. I do suggest that it is a parallel way and will keep the traveler's eyes on the desired path. As humanity advances, moral law will increasingly be considered as an aesthetic of conduct. Then man will flee from evil and error as if from dissonance and will seek the good as he would the pleasure of harmony. When symbolizing his ethic, Kant, in Stoic severity, could say, "I dreamt and thought that life was beauty, / I woke and saw that life was duty." He overlooked, however, the fact that if duty is the supreme reality, the object of his dream is contained within it, because with the clear vision of goodness, awareness of duty will give him the satisfaction of beauty.

In the soul of the savior, the missionary, the philanthropist, *comprehension of beauty* is also essential; these persons must be blessed with certain of the elements fundamental to the genius of the artist. The role that the gift of recognizing and revealing innate beauty played in the triumph of great moral revolutions cannot be overemphasized. Referring to the supreme moral revolution, Renan said, "The poetry of the precept, what causes us to cherish it, is greater than the precept itself taken as an abstract truth." The originality of Jesus' teaching does not actually lie in a literal acceptance of His doctrine, since that can be recapitulated without ever stepping outside the synagogue—in references from *Deuteronomy* to the *Talmud*—but, rather, in His teaching, in His having communicated the poetry of the precept, that is, its inner beauty.

Pale will be the glory of ages and political movements that undervalue the aesthetic worth of life, or the dissemination of that aesthetic. Christian asceticism, which perceived only one face of the ideal, excluded from its concept of perfection everything that makes life pleasant, refined, and beautiful. That narrowness of mind, spurred by man's indomitable instinct for liberty, engendered in Renaissance Italy, in one of those turbulent reversals of the human spirit, a civilization that considered moral good to be an illusion and that placed its faith in externally perceptible strength and grace. Puritanism persecuted beauty and intellectual selection; with indignation it veiled the chaste nudity of statues and affected the ugly—in manners, in clothing, and in rhetoric. This doleful sect, imposing its will through the English Parliament, declared an end to all festivities that might provoke joy and forbade planting trees that bore blossoms. Along with virtue, which it divorced from beauty, it spread a funereal shadow that still casts its pall over England, a shadow that endures in the least attractive aspects of its religion and customs. Macaulay proclaimed that he preferred the heavy lead box in which the Puritans guarded the treasure of liberty to the exquisitely carved coffer in which the court of Charles II stored its refinements. But as neither liberty nor virtue needs the protection of a lead box, we shall never value the severity of ascetics and Puritans as highly in education as we do the grace of the ancient ideal: Plato's moral harmony, the elegance and expertise with which Athenians lifted the cup of life to their lips.

If we could cast the spirit of charity in the mold of Greek elegance, we would know perfection. Such ideal harmony did live its brief moment in the world. When in its infancy the word of Christianity was carried by Saint Paul to the Greek colonies of Macedonia, Thessaly, and Philippi, and the Gospel, still pure, spread throughout those fine and spiritual colonies in which Hellenism assured spontaneity of action, it seemed that the two highest ideals in history might be be eternally joined. Saint Peter's epistolary style bears the mark of that moment when charity was Hellenized. This consonance lasted all too briefly. The harmony and serenity of the pagan concept of life grew farther and farther apart from the new ideas destined to conquer the world. But to conceive of an advance in human moral perfection, we would have to dream of the Christian ideal reconciled with the luminous joy of antiquity and imagine the Gospel again being taught in Thessaly and Philippi.

Cultivating good taste does not only mean perfecting an external form for culture, developing artistic ability, and nurturing with supreme delicacy an elegance in civilization. Good taste is also "judgment's firm reign." Benjamin-Constant Martha has defined good taste as a second consciousness that orients us and returns us to the path when the first fades or vacillates. For Walter Bagehot, a delicate sense of beauty is allied to tact and dignified behavior. "And, therefore," adds this wise commentator, "the cultivation of a fine taste tends to promote the function of a fine judgment, which is a main help in the complex world of civilized existence." If in individuals and societies this quality is occasionally joined to an absence of sentiment or morality, it is because it was cultivated in isolation and exclusivity, thus annulling the effect of moral perfectibility exerted in a cultural order that allows no faculty of mind to develop independently of others. If, however, the soul has been harmoniously stimulated, personal grace and a delicate sense of beauty will be inseparable from strength and sound intellectual judgment. This is precisely what Hippolyte Taine observed in great works of classic architecture: beauty as a palpable manifestation of solidity, and elegance allied with strength. "The same lines of the Parthenon that gratify the eye with their harmonious proportions, content the intellect with promises of eternity."

There is an organic relationship, a natural and close sympathy, that links corruption of emotion and will to the misrepresentation and distortion of bad taste. If we had the gift of entering the mysterious laboratory where souls are formed, and of reconstituting souls from the past to reveal the formula of their morality, it would be fascinating to isolate within the refined perversity of a bloodthirsty and theatrical Nero that particle of monstrous histrionics implanted by Seneca's affected rhetoric. When we recall the oratory of the French Convention, and the custom of abominable rhetorical perversion that rose up everywhere like Jacobin hair on a cat's back, we cannot fail to relate that rhetoric—in the way radii issue from a single center, or mishaps from a single madness—with absence of taste, moral vertigo, and a fanatic limitation of reason.

Few would argue that the surest effect of an aesthetic is that it teaches us, in the sphere of the relative, to distinguish the good and true from the beautiful and to accept the possibility of beauty in evil and error. But we can be ignorant of that *undeniable* truth and still believe in the sympathetic linkage of all high spiritual goals and see each of them not as the only, but as the most reliable, point of departure from which to arrive at the others.

The concept of a superior accord between good taste and morality is, then, exact: both in individuals and in societies. In the latter that relationship could be symbolized in the connection Karl Rosenkrantz claimed to have found between liberty and morality, on the one hand, and, on the other, the beauty of the human form that develops over time in some races and peoples. For this Hegelian, such beauty reflects the ennobling effect of freedom. According to his thesis, slavery disfigures as it degrades. Conversely, generations of awareness of harmonious lives imprint upon free peoples the stamp of external beauty.

In the character of a nation, the gifts derived from refined taste, the mastery of gracious modes, the delicacy of altruism, the virtue of making ideas attractive, are also identified with the "genius of propaganda"; that is, with the all-powerful gift of universality. It is a commonplace that, to a large degree, to possess these select qualities is to possess the *humanity* the French impart to the things they choose to consecrate. Ideas acquire strong, swift wings not in the icy bosom of the abstract, but in the warm and shining atmosphere of form. Whether they are widely disseminated and long lasting depends on whether the Graces have bathed them in their light. Thus it is that in the process of evolution some of the excessive entice- ments of nature that may seem to result solely from caprice— the song and bright plumage of the birds, and, to attract the pollinating insect, the color and perfume of the flowers—have actually played a practical role: their greater allure has assured that the most beautiful within a species survive over those less fortunately endowed.

A person gifted with an instinctive love of beauty undoubt- edly suffers a certain mortification in having to defend his in- stinct through a series of arguments grounded in a principle other than the independent and selfless love for beauty that is one of the bases of rational existence. Unfortunately, higher principles do not always triumph in the case of large numbers of individuals who must be taught the respect due the love in which they do not share, and who must be shown its relation- ship with other human interests. To effect this illumination, it is often necessary to combat vulgar concepts about that rela- tionship. In fact, everything that tends to soften the outlines of a society's character and customs, to excite its sense of beauty, to make of taste a refined spiritual sensitivity and of grace a universal form of behavior is, following the criterion of many adherents of severity and utilitarianism, equivalent to diminish- ing what is virile and heroic in that society, as well as its positivist and utilitarian capacities. I have read in Victor Hugo's *Les tra-*

vailleurs de la mer that when for the first time a steamship plowed the waves of the English Channel, the people of the Isle of Jersey called it anathema, following a popular tradition that considered water and fire to be irreconcilable elements fated to end in discord. Beliefs in similar enmities abound in popular thinking. If there are among you this afternoon some whose goal would be to popularize respect for the beautiful, begin by illustrating the possibility of harmonious accord among all legitimate human activities, for you will find that an easier task than to convert the multitude directly to a love of beauty for beauty's sake. If, following Pythagoras' advice, a man is to be convinced *not to drive the swallows from his house,* then you must not argue the bird's monastic grace, nor its legendary virtue, but convince the householder that the nests can remain in place without damaging the roofs on which they are built.

he concept that rational life is based on the free and harmonious evolution of our nature—and therefore includes among its primary aspirations the satisfaction that derives from contemplation of the beautiful—is opposed as a code of conduct by *utilitarianism,* in which our every action is determined by the immediate ends of self-interest.

The criticism of strict utilitarianism generally directed to the spirit of our century, in the name of the ideal and with all the rigor of anathema, is based in part upon a lack of awareness that its titanic efforts to subordinate the forces of nature to human will and to the growth of material well-being are a necessary labor that like fertilizing an exhausted soil will prepare for a future flowering of idealisms. The transitory dominance of the aspect of the utilitarian that has absorbed the vital energies of the last feverish hundred years explains, though it does not justify, many painful nostalgias and many offenses to intelligence that at times translate into nostalgia for an exalted idealization of the past and, at other times, into inevitable hopelessness in regard to the future. There is, for this reason, a procreativity, a much-welcomed vision, in the aims of a certain group of thinkers of recent generations—among whom I wish to mention once again the noble figure of Guyau—that attempts to reconcile this century's triumphs with the renewal of many of our ancient allegiances. These men have invested treasures of both love and genius in this sacred aim.

More than once, you will have heard that the prevalence of utilitarianism in the present century—to the detriment of *aestheticism* and selflessness—is due to two primary causes. One: the revelations of natural science that, according to interpreters—some adverse, some favorable—destroy all idealism at its base. The other is the universal diffusion and triumph of democratic ideas. I intend to comment only on the latter, because I am confident that your initiation into the revelations of science was such that it protects you from any danger of uninformed interpretation. Democracy has been censured for leading humankind toward a Sacred Empire of utilitarianism and, in the process, of establishing a norm of mediocrity. This vibrantly intense criticism appears in the writing of one of the most agreeable masters of the modern mind, in the seductive pages of Renan, to whom you have often heard me refer, and whom I shall frequently mention again. Read Renan, those of you who still are unfamiliar with his work, and you will revere him as I do. No one among the moderns, in my opinion, is so blessed with that art of "graceful instruction" that Anatole France considered to be divine. Even when most rigorous, Renan's analysis is like the priest's unction. Even when he instructs us to doubt, doubt is soothed by healing gentleness. His thoughts tend to expand within our soul with such ineffable echoes that they are reminiscent of a liturgical music-of-ideas. Because he is so ideally comprehensible, critics have seen in his writing the joyful skepticism of the *dilettanti* who convert the philosopher's cape into a carnival costume; but once you have penetrated his mind, you will see that the vulgar tolerance of the skeptics is as different from his as polite hospitality is from true charity.

Those questions aside, this French master believes that genuine concern for the *ideals* of the species lies in total opposition to a spirit of democracy. He believes that the concept of life in a society in which democracy prevails is progressively shaped toward the exclusive pursuit of material well-being in the guise of the greatest good for the greatest number. In his view, as democracy is the enthronement of Caliban, Ariel is necessarily vanquished in the triumph of the former. Many of Renan's opinions are substantiated in the writings of the leading contemporary philosophers, who also defend the aesthetic and the spiritual. For example, Bourget is inclined to believe that with the universal triumph of democratic institutions, civilization will lose in depth what it gains in breadth. He sees as the unavoidable consequence of democratic institutions the dominance of a mediocre individualism. "When one speaks of democracy," says the wise author of *André Cornélis*, "one speaks of the progressive growth of individualism and the concomitant decline of culture." The question planted by these harsh judgments is of lively interest to those of us who by conviction revere the results of the revolution—in our America also a kind of glorious Genesis—and by instinct revere the potential for the noble and select spirituality that should never sacrifice its serenity to the caprices of the masses. To deal with this problem, we must begin by recognizing that when democracy is not ennobled by an idealism equally as energetic as the society's material concerns, it will inevitably lead to a favored status for mediocrity. More than any other form of government, a democracy lacks protections that can efficiently ensure the inviolability of high culture. Left to itself—without the constant correction of a strong moral authority to refine and channel its inclinations in the direction of exaltation of life—democracy will gradually extinguish any superiority that does not translate into sharper and more ruthless skills in the struggles of self-interest, the self-interest that then becomes the most ignoble and brutal form of strength. Spiritual selection—the exaltation of life fostered by the altruistic stimuli of taste, art, gentility, admiration for eternal ideals, and respect for the supremacy of nobility—will be considered an indefensible weakness in societies where equality has destroyed the ruling hierarchies, whose only means of dominion is moral influence and whose strength lies in rationality: hierarchies, nevertheless, that have not been replaced by others.

True equality within societies, like true homogeneity in Nature, exists in delicate balance. The negative aspects of democracy begin to appear as soon as inequitable superiorities have been brought to a common level; the uniformity thus won, however, is merely a beginning. Affirmative values remain to be proven. And what is affirmative in democracy, indeed its glory, will consist of its ability to find effective ways to encourage the emergence and sovereignty of *true* human superiorities.

In terms of conditions here in our America, the need to define the true concept of our social regimes becomes doubly imperative. Our democratic countries have grown very swiftly, swollen by the uninterrupted growth of our cities. Large numbers of immigrants have been added to a nucleus still too weak to assimilate and channel properly this flood of humanity in ways that can be provided by a solid secular social structure, a secure political system, and deeply rooted personal values. This situation conjures up the future dangers of a democratic deterioration that will bury any notion of quality beneath the blind force of numbers, that will erase all sense of order in societal consciousness, and that in yielding hierarchical order to the vagaries of chance will necessarily lead to the triumph of unjustifiable and ignoble supremacies.

It cannot be denied that our selfish interests—in the absence of virtue—lead us to be hospitable. Some time ago the compelling need to fill the moral vacuum of vast uninhabited regions caused the famous essayist Juan Bautista Alberdi to write that in America, *gobernar es poblar* [to govern is to populate]. But this well-known maxim contains a truth that is dangerous if too narrowly interpreted, because it could lead to attributing to sheer numbers an unconditional civilizing effect. *Gobernar es poblar* is first of all governing by assimilation; later, by education and selection. If the flowering of the most desirable human activities, those existing in a high culture, requires as an indispensable condition the existence of a large and dense population, it is precisely because such numbers, giving rise to extremely complex divisions in labor, encourage the strong leadership that promotes *quality* over *number*. The anonymous masses that form the multitude are nothing in themselves. The multitude will be a tool of barbarism or civilization to the degree that it possesses or lacks the coefficient of high moral direction. There is a profound truth in Emerson's paradox that demands that nations be judged by the minority, not the majority, of their citizens. A civilization acquires its character not from a display of prosperity or material supremacy, but from the grandeur of thought and feeling possible within it. Comte has demonstrated how, in questions of intellectuality, morality, and sentiment, the accumulation of common minds can never equal the intellect of one genius, nor can the accumulation of mediocre virtues be equivalent to one shred of abnegation or heroism. By instituting universal equal rights, our democracy would be sanctioning the ignoble supremacy of numbers—unless extreme care were taken to keep firmly in mind the notion of legitimate human differences and to ensure that the authority that accompanies the popular vote is expressed not in the sophistry of absolute equality but—as articulated in Comte's *Cour de philosophie positive*—in "the consecration of a hierarchy born of freedom."

The conflict between the rule of democracy and the elevated life of the mind becomes vitally real when that form of government fails to recognize legitimate differences among us and replaces faith in *heroism*—in Carlyle's sense of the word—for a mechanistic concept of government. Any of the qualities of a civilization that lie beyond material success and economic prosperity constitute an eminence that will be razed quickly when the prevailing morality is one of mediocrity. Now that barbarism no longer unleashes its often heroic and regenerative hordes to attack the beacons of civilization, high culture must be on its guard against the mild but equally destructive effect of different peaceful, even educated, hordes: the inescapable hordes of vulgarity. Their Attila might best be personified in the character of Flaubert's M. Homais, whose heroism is mere cleverness placed at the service of an instinctive repugnance for greatness, and whose prime talent is for leveling everything that lies before him. Although immutable indifference and quantitative superiority are the normal manifestations of his strength, he is, nevertheless, capable of reaching epic levels of anger and of yielding to the impulses of aggression. Charles Morice calls such men a "fierce legion of Prudhommes who have but a single word for their motto—*Mediocrity*—and who are inspired by hatred of the extraordinary."

Given power, these Prudhommes so scaldingly satirized by Henri Monnier exert their triumphant will in the organized persecution of everything that shows the aptitude and daring for flight. Prudhommeian society will be a democracy that consecrates a Pope Nobody and crowns a King Anybody. Its citizens will despise the rebelliousness of merit. In their domain, nobility will be treated like a marble statue abandoned beside a rutted road, spattered by mud with the passing of every cart. Such mediocrities will call the dogma of vulgarity wisdom; meanness of heart, gravity; perfect adaptation to the mediocre, good judgment; and bad taste, insouciance. Following their concept of justice, they will rewrite history, substituting for the immortal either anonymity in shared oblivion, or the egalitarian memory of a Mithridates, who was said to remember the name of each of his soldiers. Their republicanism would be satisfied by granting decisive authority to the procedures of a Charles James Fox, who always tested his proposals against the opinion of a deputy whose limited faculties and crude behavior seemed most perfectly to personify the "country gentleman." With the Prudhommes, we would find ourselves on the brink of Baudelaire's "zoocracy." Shakespeare's Titania, in the act of kissing the ass's head, would serve excellently as the emblem of a Liberty who bestows her love upon the mediocre. Never, no matter how regenerative the conquest, could we suffer a worse fate!

Further, if you inflame the ubiquitous bearer of the irreverence of mediocrity, challenge him to become a hero, and make of this amiable bureaucrat a redeemer, you will have produced a rancorous and implacable hostility toward everything that is beautiful and dignified and refined in the human spirit, everything that is repugnant—more repugnant even than the brutal spilling of blood—in Jacobin tyranny. Theirs was the tribunal that judged the wisdom of Antoine Lavoisier, the genius of André Chénier, the dignity of Chrétien Malesherbes to be guilt. It is they who, among the habitual cries in the Convention, were heard to shout, "Do not trust that man, he has written a book!" And they who, attributing the ideal of democratic simplicity to Rousseau's primitive *state of nature*, could find the symbol of the discord that exists between democ-

·racy and culture in the vignette that genial sophist included in the famous diatribe he directed—in the name of morality—against the arts and sciences: an imprudent satyr who as he attempts to seize the blazing torch held by Prometheus is told by the *titan-philanthropist* that whoever touches fire shall die.

Egalitarian barbarity has not revealed its furor in the unfolding of democracy during our century, nor has it in any brutal way disturbed the serenity and independence of our intellectual culture. But, in the way that the domesticated progeny of wild beasts may have exchanged aggression for a crafty and ignoble docility, so egalitarianism, in the docility of a *tendency toward the utilitarian and the vulgar,* may be a justifiable source for criticism of nineteenth-century democracy. Every fine or sagacious mind that has analyzed democracy has also anguished over its potential effects in the political and social spheres. Indignantly and energetically rejecting the false concept of equality that erupted from the delirium of the French Revolution, contemporary intellectuals have conducted a rigorous examination of the reality and theory of democracy that will permit *you*—for it is you who will collaborate in shaping the future—to set your point of departure; not to destroy, certainly, but to enlighten the regime at present in place.

Ever since our century began to acquire an independent identity in the evolution of ideas, while German idealism was correcting the egalitarian Utopia of eighteenth-century Philosophy and aggrandizing, even if with a rather vicious Caesarcanism, the historical role reserved for individual superiority, Comte's positivism—which conceded to democratic equality nothing more than a "temporary dissolution of the old inequalities" and denied with equal conviction the final efficacy of popular rule—sought in the principles of natural classification the basis for a social classification that would replace the recently destroyed hierarchies. In the generation of Taine and Renan criticism of democratic ideas became severe. This latter modern Athenian, as you know, would not be satisfied by any equality less than that of Athens itself: "the equality of demigods." As for Taine, it was he who wrote *Les origines de la France contemporaine;* and if, on the one hand, his concept of society as an organism logically led him to reject any uniformity that was in opposition to the principle of organic dependencies and inferiorities, his extremely fine instinct for intellectual selection also led him to despise the invasion of the heights by the masses. In decrying irreverent equalization, the great voice of Carlyle had already spoken out on behalf of veneration of *heroism*—understanding, by that word, the cult of noble superiority. Emerson reflects that voice in the bosom of the most positivist of democracies. The new science speaks of choice as the basis of all progress. In art, where a sense of the exquisite finds its most natural application, resound the profound reverberations of what we might label the *estrangement* of the spirit from modern life. To hear these notes, we do not have to return to the delicate, enervated Parnassianism in which an aristocratic disdain for the present led to seclusion in the past. Among the constant inspirations of Flaubert—from whom the most democratized of our literary schools directly descends—no inspiration was more intense than hatred for the mediocrity enshrined by the leveling process, and for the irresponsible tyranny of numbers. Within contemporary Northern literature, in which we see such a lively concern for serious social questions, we often see the same idea, the same sentiment. Ibsen builds the impassioned harangue of Stockman around the statement that "the most insidious enemy of truth and freedom among us is the solid majority." And the formidable Nietzsche counterposes to the idea of an average humanity the apotheosis of souls that surge above the level of humanity like a swelling tide. Everywhere, we see an ardent desire for social adjustment that will assure an ambience of dignity and justice for *heroic* action and thought. We might even say that this aspiration provides one of the basic chords our fading century has sounded for the symphony the new century will compose.

And, nevertheless, the spirit of democracy in our civilization is a principle of life it would be futile to resist. The objections to imperfections in its *historical* form have often led to unjust appraisals of what is definitive and fruitful in it. Thus from his aristocratic wisdom Renan structures the most explicit condemnation of the basic principle of democracy: equal rights. He sees this principle as being hopelessly counter to any possibility of a reign of intellectual superiority and goes so far as to characterize the principle with this powerful image: "*the antipodes of the ways of God*—because God never intended for all to live the life of the mind to the same degree." These unfair paradoxes of the master, complemented by his famous ideal of an omnipotent oligarchy composed of wise men, are comparable to the deformed re-creation in dreams of real and fruitful thoughts that have consumed our waking hours. To reject the basic concept of democracy because, still in the process of definite formation, it has not yet reconciled its principle of equality with a strong guarantee of social selection, would be to reject the parallel and sympathetic labor of science because in the strict interpretation of a certain ideology it may occasionally have done harm to religion and poetry. Democracy and science are, in fact, the two essential pillars upon which our civilization rests. Or, as Bourget expressed it, "the two great 'crafters' of our future destinies." In them, in the words of Saint Paul, *we are, we live, we move* [in eo movemur, vivimus et sumus]. It is, then, illogical to believe, as Renan does, that we will achieve a stronger dedication to moral superiority and logical hierarchies, and to effective utilization of the supreme gifts of intelligence and will, through the *destruction* of democratic equality, when what we must do is plan for the *better application* and reform of democracy. We must work toward the end that the idea of necessary inferiorities, the notion of true superiorities, and the conscious but spontaneous cultivation of everything that in the eyes of reason increases human worth will gradually take form in the feelings and practices of the people.

Considered in relation to this undertaking, popular education assumes, as has always been the case when planning for the future, a supreme importance. It is in our schools that we first attempt to mold the intractable clay of the masses; it is in the schools where we see the first and most generous manifestation of social equality; and it is the schools that make learning, the most efficacious means of self-betterment, available to all. The school must be worthy of such a noble charge. It must set the goals for a worthwhile education: a sense of order, a concept of and desire for justice, and a sense of legitimate moral authority.

No concept is so easily confused and nullified in the mind of the people as the one that teaches that democratic equality may mean an equal *potential for* but never an equal *realization of* influence and prestige among the citizens of an organized society. Among all citizens there is an identical right to aspire to the moral superiorities that must provide a rationale and a basis for actual superiorities. But only those who truly possess the former will ever be granted the reward of the latter. The true and noble concept of equality rests on the belief that all rational beings are gifted by nature with faculties that make them capable of growing in nobility. It is the duty of the State to provide all members of the society with the unspecified conditions that will lead to their perfection. It is the duty of the State to provide the necessary conditions that will lead to the development of human superiorities wherever they exist. In this way, if all are granted initial equality, subsequent inequality will be justified, since it will bear the sanction either of the mysterious selection of Nature or of meritorious effort of will. Considered in this way, democratic equality, far from conflicting with selection in customs and ideas, becomes the most efficient—in fact, the *providential*—instrument in spiritual selection. It will be favored by everything that favors the dominance of intelligent energy. This is what de Tocqueville meant when he said that poetry, eloquence, the spiritual graces, flashes of imagination, profundity of thought, "all those gifts of the soul indiscriminately apportioned by heaven," were collaborators in the work of democracy and served it, even when they were on the side of its adversaries, because they underscored the natural, not the inherited, grandeur of which our spirit is capable. Emulation, that most powerful of all spurs to action—in vigor of thought as well as other human activities—demands two conditions: in the beginning, equality; and, as a final objective, the inequality that works to the advantage of the best and most apt. Only a democratic regime can reconcile these two conditions without allowing them to degenerate into a leveling egalitarianism, and, at the same time, to strive for a beautiful ideal of perfectibility: a future equality gained by ascent to a common standard of culture.

Rationally conceived, democracy always includes an indispensable element of aristocracy, a means of establishing the superiority of the finest, achieved through free consent. A democracy, like an aristocracy, will recognize the distinction of quality; but it will favor truly superior qualities—those of virtue, character, and mind—and will not attempt to immobilize them in a class system that maintains the execrable privilege of caste. Democracy ceaselessly revitalizes the ruling aristocracy in the living springs of the people and makes justice and love the condition for its acceptance. Thus, by recognizing that the basis for all progress lies in selection and in the dominance of the most highly gifted, democracy excludes from the universal law of life the humiliation and pain that in the rivalries of nature and those of other social organizations are the hard lot of the loser. As Fouillée has brilliantly observed, "The great law of natural selection will continue to function in our societies, although more and more it will be freely effected." The odious nature of traditional aristocracies derives from the fact that they were inherently unjust; they were, further, oppressive, because their authority was imposed. Today we know that there is no limitation to human equality except for the authority of intelligence and virtue freely and universally agreed upon. But we also know that limits do, in reality, exist. In addition, our Christian concept of life teaches us that moral superiorities, which are a justification for rights, are actually a source of responsibilities and that every superior mind is responsible to all others in direct proportion to the degree it exceeds them in its capacity to effect good. The antiegalitarianism of Nietzsche— which has cut so deeply through what we could call our *modern literature of ideas*—has imbued his staunch defense of the rights he believes to be implicit in superior human beings with abominable reactionism. Denying all fraternity, all pity, he places in the heart of his deified *superman* a satanic scorn for the helpless and the weak. For those favored with will and strength, he legitimizes the measures of the executioner. And as the logical consummation he observes that "society does not exist for itself, but for its elect." This monstrous concept is, certainly, no model to oppose to the false egalitarianism that aspires to bring everyone down to a common level of vulgarity. Fortunately, as long as there exists in the world the possibility of placing together two pieces of wood in the form of a cross— that is, always—humanity will continue to believe that love is the basis of every stable order and that hierarchical superiority in that order can derive only from a superior capacity to love.

As a source of inexhaustible moral inspirations the new science demonstrates to us, in clarifying the old physical laws, how the democratic principle can be reconciled in the social structure with an "aristarchy" of morality and culture. On the one hand—as Henri Bérenger has shown in his admirable book—the laws of science tend to sanction and strengthen the spirit of democracy by revealing the greatness of the collective effort, the value of the labor of the most insignificant contributor, and the enormity of the role reserved for the anonymous and obscure in any stage of universal evolution. No less than Christian revelation, this new revelation enhances the dignity of the humble, in nature crediting the infinitesimal nummulite and bryozoan in the depths of the oceanic abyss with the construction of geological strata; seeing in the oscillations of the formless, primitive cell all the impulses of ascendant organic life; in our psychic lives, illustrating the powerful role we must grant to vague and undefined phenomena—even fleeting perceptions of which we are not fully aware. In sociology and history, these new revelations make restitution to the often self-sacrificing heroism of the masses by granting them their previously unvoiced share of the glory accorded to individual heroes. Science clearly demonstrates how countless workshop and laboratory investigations conducted by unheralded and long-forgotten workers paved the way for major discoveries made by geniuses.

But at the same time that it confirms the eternal efficacy of the collective effort and dignifies the participation of ignored collaborators, science proves that hierarchical order is a necessary condition for all progress. Relationships of dependence and subordination among individual components of society, and within the individual himself, are a principle of life. Finally, that hierarchy is essential to the universal law of *imitation*. And when that law is applied to perfecting society, living and influential models must be present to elevate social norms by the increasing prevalence of superior example.

To demonstrate that both these universal teachings of science may be translated into fact, and may be reconciled within the structure and spirit of a society, we need only insist on the concept of a noble and just democracy: a democracy directed by the idea that true human superiorities exist, a democracy in which the supremacy of intelligence and virtue—the only justifiable restrictions for a meritorious equality—receives its authority and prestige from free men and filters down to the masses as the beneficial effusion of love.

As Bérenger observes in the book I have already mentioned, at the same time that the two major results of observing natural order are being reconciled, a harmony will be effected in such a society between the two historical impulses that have shaped the essential characteristics and regulating principles of our civilization. Our egalitarian sense, in fact, was born of Christianity—vitiated by a certain ascetic scorn for spiritual selection and culture. From classic civilizations were born a sense for order and hierarchy and an almost religious respect for genius—vitiated by a certain aristocratic disdain for the humble and the weak. The future will synthesize these two archetypal patterns into an immortal plan. Then democracy shall definitely have triumphed. And though the threat of its ignoble leveling effect may justify the angry protests and bitter melancholy of those who believe its triumph will mean the sacrifice of all intellectual distinctions, all hope for art, all refinement in life, democracy, even more than the old aristocracies, will offer inviolable safeguards for cultivating the flowers of the soul that wither and die in an atmosphere of vulgarity.

The inextricably linked concepts of utilitarianism as a concept of human destiny and egalitarian mediocrity as a norm for social relationships compose the formula for what Europe has tended to call the spirit of *Americanism*. It is impossible to ponder either inspiration for social conduct, or to compare them with their opposites, without their inevitable association with that formidable and productive democracy to our North. Its display of prosperity and power is dazzling testimony to the efficacy of its institutions and to the guidance of its concepts. If it has been said that "utilitarianism" is the word for the spirit of the English, then the United States can be considered the embodiment of the word. And the Gospel of that word is spread everywhere through the good graces of its material miracles. Spanish America is not, in this regard, entirely a land of heathens. That powerful federation is effecting a kind of moral conquest among us. Admiration for its greatness and power is making impressive inroads in the minds of our leaders and, perhaps even more, in the impressionable minds of the masses, who are awed by its incontrovertible victories. And from admiring to imitating is an easy step. A psychologist will say that admiration and conviction are passive modes of imitation. "The main seat of the imitative part of our nature is our belief," said Bagehot. Common sense and experience should in themselves be enough to establish this simple relationship. We imitate what we believe to be superior or prestigious. And this is why the vision of an America de-Latinized of its own will, without threat of conquest, and reconstituted in the image and likeness of the North, now looms in the nighmares of many who are genuinely concerned about our future. This vision is the impetus behind an abundance of similar carefully thought-out designs and explains the continuous flow of proposals for innovation and reform. We have our *USA-mania.* It must be limited by the boundaries our reason and sentiment jointly dictate.

When I speak of boundaries, I do not suggest absolute negation. I am well aware that we find our inspirations, our enlightenment, our teachings, in the example of the strong; nor am I unaware that intelligent attention to external events is singularly fruitful in the case of a people still in the process of forming its national entity. I am similarly aware that by per-severing in the educational process we hope to modulate the elements of society that must be adapted to new exigencies of civilization and new opportunities in life, thus balancing the forces of heritage and custom with that of innovation. I do not, however, see what is to be gained from denaturalizing the char-acter—the *personality*—of a nation, from imposing an iden-tification with a foreign model, while sacrificing irreplaceable uniqueness. Nor do I see anything to be gained from the in-genuous belief that identity can somehow be achieved through artificial and improvised imitation. Michelet believed that the mindless transferral of what is natural and spontaneous in one society to another where it has neither natural nor historical roots was like attempting to introduce a dead organism into a living one by simple implantation. In a social structure, as in literature and art, forced imitation will merely distort the con-figuration of the model. The misapprehension of those who believe they have reproduced the character of a human collec-tivity in its essence, the living strength of its spirit, as well as the secret of its triumphs and prosperity, and have exactly re-produced the mechanism of its institutions and the external form of its customs, is reminiscent of the delusion of naïve stu-dents who believe they have achieved the genius of their master when they have merely copied his style and characteristics.

In such a futile effort there is, furthermore, an inexpressible ignobility. Eager mimicry of the prominent and the powerful, the successful and the fortunate, must be seen as a kind of po-litical *snobbery;* and a servile abdication—like that of some snobs condemned by Thackeray in *The Book of Snobs* to be sati-rized for all eternity—lamentably consumes the energies of those who are not blessed by nature or fortune but who impo-tently ape the caprices and foibles of those at the peak of so-ciety. Protecting our *internal* independence—independence of personality and independence of judgment—is a basic form of self-respect. Treatises on ethics often comment on one of Cicero's moral precepts, according to which one of our responsibilities as human beings is zealously to protect the uniqueness of our personal character—whatever in it that is different and formative—while always respecting Nature's primary impulse: that the order and harmony of the world are based on the broad distribution of her gifts. The truth of this precept would seem even greater when applied to the character of human societies. Perhaps you will hear it said that there is no distinctive mark or characteristic of the present ordering of our peoples that is worth struggling to maintain. What may perhaps be lacking in our collective character is a sharply defined "personality." But in lieu of an absolutely distinct and autonomous particularity, we Latin Americans have a heritage of race, a great ethnic tradition, to maintain, a sacred place in the pages of history that depends upon us for its continuation. Cosmopolitanism, which we must respect as a compelling requisite in our formation, includes fidelity both to the past and to the formative role that the genius of our race must play in recasting the American of tomorrow.

More than once it has been observed that the great epochs of history, the most luminous and fertile periods in the evolution of humankind, are almost always the result of contemporaneous but conflicting forces that through the stimulus of concerted opposition preserve our interest in life, a fascination that would pale in the placidity of absolute conformity. So it was that the most genial and civilizing of cultures turned upon an axis supported by the poles of Athens and Sparta. America must continue to maintain the dualism of its original composition, which re-creates in history the classic myth of the two eagles released simultaneously from the two poles in order that each should reach the limits of its domain at the same moment. Genial and competitive diversity does not exclude but, rather, tolerates, and even in many aspects favors, solidarity. And if we

[73]

could look into the future and see the formula for an eventual harmony, it would not be based upon the *unilateral imitation*— as Gabriel Tarde would say—of one people by another, but upon a mutual exchange of influences, and the fortuitous fusion of the attributes that gave each its special glory.

In addition, a dispassionate examination of the civilization that some consider to be the only perfect model will reveal no less powerful reasons to temper the enthusiasms of those who demand idolatrous devotion, reasons other than those based on the thesis that to reject everything original is both unworthy and unjustifiable. And now I come to the direct relation between the theme of my talk and the spirit of imitation.

Any criticism of the Americans to our north should always be accompanied, as in the case of any worthy opponent, with the chivalrous salute that precedes civilized combat. And I make that bow sincerely. But to ignore a North American's defects would seem to me as senseless as to deny his good qualities. Born—calling upon the paradox that Baudelaire employed in a different context—with the *innate experience* of freedom, they have remained faithful to the laws of their origins and with the precision and sureness of a mathematical progression have developed the basic principles of their formation. Subsequently, their history is characterized by a uniformity that, although it may lack diversity in skills and values, does possess the intellectual beauty of logic. The traces of their presence will never be erased from the annals of human rights. From tentative essays and utopian visions, they were the first to evoke our modern ideal of liberty, forging imperishable bronze and living reality from concepts. With their example they have demonstrated the possibility of imposing the unyielding authority of a republic upon an enormous national organism. With their federation they have demonstrated—recalling de Tocqueville's felicitous expression—how the brilliance and power of large states can be reconciled with the happiness and peace of the small. Some of the boldest strokes in the panorama of this century, deeds that will be recorded through all time, are theirs. Theirs, too, the glory of having fully established—by amplifying the strongest note of moral beauty in our civilization—the grandeur and power of work, that sacred power that antiquity degraded to the abjectness of slave labor, and that today we identify with the highest expression of human dignity, founded on the awareness of its intrinsic worth. Strong, tenacious, believing that inactivity is ignominious, they have placed in the hands of the mechanic in his shop and the farmer in his field the mythic club of Hercules and have given human nature a new and unexpected beauty by girding onto it the blacksmith's leather apron. Each of them marches forward to conquer life in the same way the first Puritans set out to tame the wilderness. Persevering devotees of that cult of individual energy that makes each man the author of his own destiny, they have modeled their society on an imaginary assemblage of Crusoes who, after gaining their crude strength by looking out for their self-interests, set to weaving the stout cloth of their society. Without sacrificing the sovereign concept of individualism, they have at the same time created from the spirit of association the most admirable instrument of their grandeur and empire. Similarly, from the sum of individual strengths subordinated to a plan of research, philanthropy, and industry, they have achieved marvelous results that are all the more remarkable, considering that they were obtained while maintaining the absolute integrity of personal autonomy. There is in these North Americans a lively and insatiable curiosity and an avid thirst for enlightenment. Professing their reverence for public education with an obsessiveness that resembles monomania—glorious and productive as it may be—they have made the school the hub of their prosperity, and a child's soul the most valued of all precious commodities. Although their culture is far from being refined or spiritual, it is admirably efficient as long as it is directed to the practical goal of realizing an immediate end. They have not added a single general law, a single principle, to the storehouse of scientific knowledge. They have, however, worked magic through the marvels of their application of general knowledge. They have grown tall as giants in the domains of utility; and in the steam engine and electric generator they have given the world billions of invisible slaves to serve the human Aladdin, increasing a hundredfold the power of the magic lamp. The extent of their greatness and strength will amaze generations to come. With their prodigious skill for improvisation, they have invented a way to speed up time; and by the power of will in one day they have conjured up from the bosom of absolute solitude a culture equal to the work of centuries. The liberty of Puritanism, still shedding its light from the past, joined to that light the heat of a piety that lives today. Along with factories and schools, their strong hands have also raised the churches from which rise the prayers of many millions of free consciences. They have been able to save from the shipwreck of all idealisms the highest idealism, keeping alive the tradition of a religion that although it may not fly on wings of a delicate and profound spiritualism does, at least, amid the harshness of the utilitarian tumult, keep a firm grip on the reins of morality. Surrounded by the refinements of civilized life, they have also been able to maintain a certain robust primitivism. They have a pagan cult of health, of skill, of strength; they temper and refine the precious instrument of will in muscle; and obliged, by their insatiable appetite for dominance, to cultivate all human activities with obsessive energy, they build an athlete's torso in which to shelter the heart of free man. And from the concord of their civilization, from the harmonious mobility of their culture, sounds a dominant note of optimism and confidence and faith that expands their hearts; they advance toward the future under the power of a stubborn and arrogant expectation. This is the note of Longfellow's "Excelsior" and "A Psalm of Life," which their poets, in the philosophy of strength and action, have advocated as an infallible balm against all bitterness.

Thus their titanic greatness impresses even those who have been forewarned by the enormous excesses of their character or the recent violence of their history. As for me, you have already seen that, although I do not love them, I admire them. I admire them, first of all, for their formidable strength of *volition* and, as Philarète Chasles said of their English forebears, I bow before the "school of will and work" they have instituted.

In the beginning was Action. A future historian of that powerful republic could begin the still-to-be-concluded Genesis of their national existence with these famous words from *Faust*. Their genius, like the universe of the Dynamists, could be defined as *force in motion*. Above all else, they have the capacity, the enthusiasm, and the blessed vocation for action. Will is the chisel that has sculptured these peoples in hard stone. Their outstanding characteristics are the two manifestations of the power of will: originality and boldness. Their history, in its entirety, has been marked by paroxysms of vigorous activity. Their typical figure, like Nietzsche's *superman,* is named *I Will It.* If something saves him, collectively, from vulgarity, it is that extraordinary show of energy that leads to achievement and that allows him to invest even the struggles of self-interest and materialism with a certain aura of epic grandeur. Thus Paul Bourget could say that the speculators of Chicago and Minneapolis are like heroic warriors whose skills of attack and defense are comparable to those of Napoleon's veteran *grognards.* And this supreme energy that seems to permit North American genius—audacious and hypnotic as it is—to cast spells and the power of suggestion over the Fates is to be found even in those peculiarities of their civilization that we consider exceptional or divergent. For example, no one will deny that Edgar Allan Poe is one such anomalous and rebellious individual. He is of the elect who resist assimilation into the national soul, a person who successfully, if in infinite solitude, struggled among his fellows for self-expression. And yet—as Baudelaire has so tellingly pointed out—the basic characteristic of Poe's heroes is still the superhuman persistence, the indomitable stamina, of their will. When Poe conceived Ligeia, the most mysterious and adorable of his creatures, he symbolized in the inextinguishable light of her eyes the hymn of the triumph of Will over Death.

With my sincere recognition of all that is luminous and great in its genius, I have won the right to complete a fair appraisal of this powerful nation; one vital question, however, remains to be answered. Is that society achieving, or at least partially achieving, the concept of rational conduct that satisfies the legitimate demands of intellectual and moral dignity? Will this be the society destined to create the closest approximation of the "perfect state"? Does the feverish restlessness that seems to magnify the activity and intensity of their lives have a truly worthwhile objective, and does that stimulus justify their impatience?

Herbert Spencer, voicing his sincere and noble tribute to American democracy at a banquet in New York City, identified this same unrestrainable restiveness as the fundamental characteristic of the lives of North Americans, an agitation manifest in their infinite passion for work and their drive toward material expansion in all its forms. And then he observed that such an atmosphere of activity exclusively subordinated to the immediate proposals of utility denoted a concept of life that might well be acceptable as a provisional quality of a civilization, or as the preliminary stage of a culture. Such a concept, however, demands subsequent revision, for unless that tendency is curbed, the result will be to convert utilitarian work into an end, into the supreme goal of life, when rationally it can be only one among numbers of elements that facilitate the har-

monious development of our being. Then Spencer added that
it was time to preach to North Americans the "gospel of relaxa-
tion." And as we identify the ultimate meaning of those words
with the classic concept of *otium,* as it was dignified by the
moralists of antiquity, we would include among the chapters of
gospel those tireless workers should heed, everything concerned with the ideal, the use of time for other than selfish
purposes, and any meditation not directed toward the immediate ends of utility.

North American life, in fact, perfectly describes the vicious
circle identified by Pascal: the fervent pursuit of well-being that
has no object beyond itself. North American prosperity is as
great as its inability to satisfy even an average concept of human
destiny. In spite of its titanic accomplishments and the great
force of will that those accomplishments represent, and in spite
of its incomparable triumphs in all spheres of material success,
it is nevertheless true that as an entity this civilization creates a
singular impression of insufficiency and emptiness. And when
following the prerogative granted by centuries of evolution
dominated by the dignity of classicism and Christianity we ask,
what is its directing principle, what its ideal *substratum,* what
the ultimate goal of the present Positivist interests surging
through that formidable mass, we find nothing in the way of a
formula for a definitive ideal but the same eternal preoccupation with material triumphs. Having drifted from the traditions that set their course, the peoples of this nation have not
been able to replace the inspiring idealism of the past with a
high and selfless concept of the future. They live for the immediate reality, for the present, and thereby subordinate all their
activity to the egoism of personal and collective well-being. Of
the sum of their riches and power could be said what Bourget
said of the intelligence of the Marquis de Norbert, a figure in
one of his books: that it is like a well-laid fire to which no one
has set a match. What is lacking is the kindling spark that causes

the flame of a vivifying and exciting ideal to blaze from the abundant but unlighted wood. Not even national egoism, lacking a higher motivation, not even exclusiveness and pride of nationhood, which is what in antiquity transfigured and exalted the prosaic severity of Roman life, can engender glimmers of idealism and beauty in a people in whom cosmopolitan confusion and the *atomism* of a poorly understood democracy impede the formation of a true national consciousness.

It could be said that when the Positivism of the mother country was transmitted to her emancipated children in America, it suffered a distilling process that filtered out the emollient idealism, reducing it to the harshness that previous excessive passion and satire had attributed to English Positivism. But beneath the hard utilitarian shell, beneath the mercantile cynicism, beneath the Puritanical severity, the English spirit masks—you must never doubt it—a poetic genius and a profound veneration for sensitivity. All this, in Taine's opinion, reveals that the primitive, the Germanic, essence of that people, later diluted by the pressures of conquest and commercial activities, was one of an extraordinary exaltation of sentiment. The American spirit did not inherit the ancestral poetic instinct that bursts like a crystalline stream from the heart of Britannic rock when smitten by an artistic Moses. In the institution of their aristocracy—as anachronistic and unjust as it may be in the realm of politics—the English people possess a high and impregnable bulwark against the attacks of mercantilism and the encroachment of the prosaic. This bulwark is so high and so impregnable that Taine himself states that, since the age of the Greek city-states, history has not seen an example of a way of life more propitious to heightening a sense of human nobility. In the ambience of American democracy, the spirit of vulgarity encounters no barriers to slow its rising waters, and it spreads and swells as if flooding across an endless plain.

Sensibility, intelligence, customs—everything in that enormous land is characterized by a radical ineptitude for selectivity which, along with the mechanistic nature of its materialism and its politics, nurtures a profound disorder in anything having to do with idealism. It is all too easy to follow the manifestations of that ineptitude, beginning with the most external and apparent, then arriving at those that are more essential and internal. Prodigal with his riches—because in his appetites, as Bourget has astutely commented, there is no trace of Molière's miserly Harpagon—the North American has with his wealth achieved all the satisfaction and vanity that come with sumptuous magnificence—but good taste has eluded him. In such an atmosphere, true art can exist only in the form of individual rebellion. Emerson and Poe, in that situation, are like plants cruelly uprooted from their natural soil by the spasms of a geologic catastrophe. Bourget, in *Outre mer,* speaks of the solemnity with which the word *art* trembles on the lips of the North Americans who have courted fortune. In such sycophancy, the hearty and righteous heroes of *self-help* hope to crown, by assimilating refinement, the labor of their tenaciously won eminence. But never have they conceived of the divine activity they so emphatically profess as anything other than a new way to satisfy their pervading restiveness, and as a trophy for their vanity. They ignore in art all that is selfless and selective. They ignore it, in spite of the munificence with which private fortunes are employed to stimulate an appreciation of beauty; in spite of the splendid museums and exhibitions their cities boast; in spite of the mountains of marble and bronze they have sculptured into statues for their public squares. And if a word may some day characterize their taste in art, it will be a word that negates art itself: the grossness of affectation, the ignorance of all that is subtle and exquisite, the cult of false grandeur, the *sensationalism* that excludes the serenity that is irreconcilable with the pace of a feverish life.

The idealism of beauty does not fire the soul of a descendant of austere Puritans. Nor does the idealism of truth. He scorns as vain and unproductive any exercise of thought that does not yield an immediate result. He does not bring to science a selfless thirst for truth, nor has he ever shown any sign of revering science for itself. For him, research is merely preparation for a utilitarian application. His grandiose plans to disseminate the benefits of popular education were inspired in the noble goal of communicating rudimentary knowledge to the masses; but although those plans promote the growth of education, we have seen no sign that they contain any imperative to enhance selective education, or any inclination to aid in allowing excellence to rise above general mediocrity. Thus the persistent North American war against ignorance has resulted in a universal *semi*-culture, accompanied by the diminution of high culture. To the same degree that basic ignorance has diminished in that gigantic democracy, wisdom and genius have correspondingly disappeared. This, then, is the reason that the trajectory of their intellectual activity is one of decreasing brilliance and originality. While in the period of independence and the formation of their nation many illustrious names emerged to expound both the thought and the will of that people, only a half century later de Tocqueville could write of them, *the gods have departed.* It is true, however, that even as de Tocqueville was writing his masterpiece, the rays of a glorious pleiad of universal magnitude in the intellectual history of this century were still beaming forth from Boston, the *Puritan citadel,* the city of learned traditions. But who has come along to perpetuate the bequest of a William Ellery Channing, an Emerson, a Poe? The bourgeois leveling process, ever-swifter in its devastation, is tending to erase what little character remains of their precarious intellectualism. For some time now North American literature has not been borne to heights where it can be perceived by the rest of the world. And today the most genuine representation of American taste in belle lettres is to be found in the gray pages of a journalism that bears little resemblance to that of the days of the *Federalist*.

In the area of morality, the mechanistic thrust of utilitarianism has been somewhat regulated by the balance wheel of a strong religious tradition. We should not, nevertheless, conclude that this tradition has led to true principles of selflessness. North American religion, a derivation from and exaggeration of English religion, actually serves to aid and enforce penal law that will relinquish its hold only on the day it becomes possible to grant to moral authority the religious authority envisioned by John Stuart Mill. Benjamin Franklin represents the highest point in North American morality: a philosophy of conduct whose ideals are grounded in the normality of honesty and the utility of prudence. His is a philosophy that would never give rise to either sanctity or heroism, one that although it may—like the cane that habitually supports its originator—lend conscience support along the everyday paths of life is a frail staff indeed when it comes to scaling the peaks. And these are the heights; consider the reality to be found in the valleys. Even were the moral criterion to sink no lower than Franklin's honest and moderate utilitarianism, the inevitable consequence—already revealed in de Tocqueville's sagacious observation—of a society educated in such limitations of duty would not inevitably be that state of proud and magnificent decadence that reveals the proportions of the satanic beauty of evil during the dissolution of empires; it would, instead, result in a kind of pallid and mediocre materialism and, ultimately, the lassitude of a lusterless enervation resulting from the quiet winding-down of all the mainsprings of moral life. In a society whose precepts tend to place the demonstration of self-sacrifice and virtue outside the realm of obligation, the bounds of that obligation will constantly be pushed back. And the school of material prosperity—always an ordeal for republican austerity—that captures minds today has carried the simplistic concept of rational conduct even farther. In their frankness other codes have surpassed even Franklin as an expression of the national wisdom. And it is not more than five years ago that in all of North America's cities public opinion consecrated, with the most unequivocal demonstration of popular and critical acclaim, the new moral law: from the Boston of the Puritans, Orison Swett Mardin wrote a learned book entitled *Pushing to the Front*, solemnly announcing that *success* should be considered the supreme goal of life. His "revelation" echoed even in the bosom of Christian fellowship, and once was cited as being comparable to Thomas à Kempis' *The Imitation of Christ*.

Public life, of course, does not escape the consequences of the spread of the germ of disorganization harbored in the entrails of that society. Any casual observer of its political customs can relate how the obsession of utilitarian interests tends progressively to enervate and impoverish the sense of righteousness in the hearts of its citizens. Civic valor, that venerable Hamiltonian virtue, is a forgotten sword that lies rusting among the cobwebs of tradition. Venality, which begins in the polling places, spreads through the workings of the institution. A government of mediocrity discourages the emulation that exalts character and intelligence and relates those qualities to the efficacy of power. Democracy, which consistently has resisted the regulator of a noble and instructive notion of human excellence, has always tended toward an abominable slavishness to numbers that undervalues the greatest moral benefits of liberty and nullifies respect for the dignity of others. Today, furthermore, a formidable force is rising up to emphasize the absolutism of numbers. The political influence of a plutocracy represented by the all-powerful allies of the trust, the monopolizers of production and masters of the economy, is undoubtedly one of the most significant features in the present physiognomy of that great nation. The formation of this plutocracy has caused some to recall, with good reason, the rise of the arrogant and wealthy class that in the waning days of the Roman republic was one of the visible signs of the decline of liberty and the tyranny of the Caesars. And the exclusive concern for material gain—the numen of that civilization—imposes its logic on political life, as well as on all other areas of activity, granting the greatest prominence to Alphonse Daudet's bold and astute *Struggle-for-lifer,* become, by dint of brutal efficiency, the supreme personification of national energy: a postulant for Emerson's *representative man,* or for Taine's *personnage régnant* [leading personage].

There is a second impulse corresponding to the one that in the life of the spirit is speeding toward utilitarian egoism and the disintegration of idealism, and that is the physical impulse the multitudes and the initiatives of an astounding population explosion are pushing Westward toward the boundless territory that throughout the period of the Independence was still a mystery hidden by the forests of the Mississippi. In fact, it is in this extemporaneous West—beginning to be so formidable to the interests of the original Atlantic states, and threatening in the near future to demand its hegemony—that we find the most faithful representation of contemporary North American life. It is in the West that the definitive results, the logical and natural fruits, of the spirit that has led this powerful democracy away from its origins stand out so clearly, allowing the observer to picture the face of the immediate future of this great nation. As a representative type, the Yankee and Virginian have been replaced by the tamer of the only-yesterday-deserted Plains, those settlers of whom Michel Chevalier said, prophetically, a half-century ago, "the last shall be first." In that man of the West, a utilitarianism void of any idealism, a kind of universal *in*definition and the leveling process of an ill-conceived democracy will reach their ultimate triumph. Everything noble in that civilization, everything that binds it to magnanimous memories and supports its historic dignity—the heritage of the *May-*

flower, the memory of patrician Virginians and New England gentry, the spirit of the citizens and the legislators of the emancipation—will live on in the original States, there where in Boston and Philadelphia "the palladium of Washingtonian tradition" is still upheld. It is Chicago that now rears its head to rule. And its confidence in its superiority over the original Atlantic states is based on the conviction that they are too reactionary, too European, too traditional. History confers no titles when the election process entails auctioning off the purple.

To the degree that the generic utilitarianism of that civilization assumes more defined, more open, and more limiting characteristics, the intoxication of material prosperity increases the impatience of its children to propagate that doctrine and enshrine it with the historical importance of a Rome. Today, North Americans openly aspire to preeminence in universal culture, to leadership in ideas; they consider themselves the forgers of a type of civilization that will endure forever. The semi-ironic speech that René Lefebvre Laboulaye places in the mouth of a student in his Americanized Paris to signify the superiority that experience has conceded to whatever favors the pride of nationalism would today be accepted by any patriotic North American as absolute truth. At the base of the Americans' open rivalry with Europe there is an ingenuous disdain, and the profound conviction that Americans will in a very brief time obscure the intellectual superiority and glory of Europe, once again fulfilling in the evolution of human civilization the harsh law of the ancient mysteries in which the initiate always killed his initiator. It would be futile to attempt to convince a North American that, although the contribution his nation has made to the evolution of liberty and utility has undoubtedly been substantial, and should rightly qualify as a universal contribution, indeed, as a contribution to *humanity,* it is not so great as to cause the axis of the world to shift in the direction of a new Capitol. It would be similarly futile to attempt to convince him that the enduring achievements of the European Aryans, who dwelt along the civilizing shores of the Mediterranean that more than three thousand years ago jubilantly displayed the garland of its Hellenic cities—achievements that survived until today, and whose traditions and teachings we still adhere to—form a sum that cannot be equaled by the formula *Washington plus Edison.* Given the opportunity, they would gladly revise *Genesis,* hoping to gain a place "in the beginning." But, in addition to the relative modesty of their role in the enlightenment of humanity, their very character denies them the possibility of hegemony. Nature has not gifted them either with a genius for persuasion or with the vocation of the apostle. They lack the supreme gift of *amiability,* given the highest meaning of the word, that is, the extraordinary power of sympathy that enables nations endowed by Providence with the gift and responsibility for educating to instill in their culture something of the beauty of classic Greece, beauty of which all cultures hope to find some trace. That civilization may abound—undoubtedly it does abound—in proposals and productive examples. It may inspire admiration, amazement, and respect. But it is difficult to believe that when a stranger glimpses their enormous symbol from the high seas—Bartholdi's Statue of Liberty, triumphantly lifting her torch high above the port of New York City—it awakens in his soul the deep and religious feeling that must have been evoked in the diaphanous nights of Attica by the sight of Athena high upon the Acropolis, her bronze sword, glimpsed from afar, gleaming in the pure and serene atmosphere.

I want each of you to be aware that when in the name of the rights of the spirit I resist the mode of North American utilitarianism, which they want to impose on us as the summa and model of civilization, I do not imply that everything they have achieved in the sphere of what we might call *the interests of the soul* has been entirely negative. Without the arm that levels and constructs, the arm that serves the noble work of the mind would not be free to function. Without a certain material well-being, the realm of the spirit and the intellect could not exist. The aristocratic idealism of Renan accepts this fact when it exalts—in relation to the moral concerns of the species and its future spiritual selection—the importance of the utilitarian work of this century. "To rise above necessity," the master adds, "is to be redeemed." In the remote past, the effects of the prosaic and self-interested actions of the merchant who first put one people in contact with others were of incalculable value in disseminating ideas, since such contacts were an effective way to enlarge the scope of intelligence, to polish and refine customs, even, perhaps, to advance morality. The same positive force reappears later, propitiating the highest idealism of civilization. According to Paul de Saint-Victor, the gold accumulated by the mercantilism of the Italian republics financed the Renaissance. Ships returning from the lands of the Thousand and One Nights laden with spices and ivory to fill the storehouses of the Florentine merchants made it possible for Lorenzo de Medici to renew the Platonic feast. History clearly demonstrates a reciprocal relationship between the progress of utilitarianism and idealism. And in the same way that utility often serves as a strong shield for the ideal, frequently (as long as it is not specifically intended) the ideal evokes the useful. Bagehot, for example, observed that mankind might never have enjoyed the positive benefits of navigation had there not in primitive ages been idle dreamers—surely misunderstood by their contemporaries—who were intrigued by contemplating the movement of the planets. This law of harmony teaches us to respect the arm that tills the inhospitable soil of the prosaic and the ordinary. Ultimately, the work of North American Positivism will serve the cause of Ariel. What that Cyclopean nation, with its sense of the useful and its admirable aptitude for mechanical invention, has achieved directly in the way of material well-being, other peoples, or they themselves in the future, will effectively incorporate into the process of selection. This is how the most precious and fundamental of the acquisitions of the spirit—the alphabet, which lends immortal wings to the word—was born in the very heart of Canaanite trading posts, the discovery of a mercantile civilization that used it for exclusively financial purposes, never dreaming that the genius of superior races would transfigure it, converting it into a means of communicating mankind's purest and most luminous essence. The relationship between material good and moral and intellectual good is, then, according to an analogy offered by Fouillée, nothing more than a new aspect of the old equivalence of forces; and, in the same way that motion is transformed into heat, elements of spiritual excellence may also be obtained from material benefits.

As yet, however, North American life has not offered us a new example of that incontestable relationship, nor even afforded a glimpse of a glorious future. Our confidence and our opinion must incline us to believe, however, that in an inferred future their civilization is destined for excellence. Considering that under the scourge of intense activity the very brief time separating them from their dawn has witnessed a sufficient expenditure of life forces to effect a great evolution, their past and present can only be the prologue to a promising future. Everything indicates that their evolution is still very far from definitive. The assimilative energy that has allowed them to preserve a certain uniformity and a certain generic character in spite of waves of ethnic groups very different from those that have until now set the tone for their national identity will be vitiated in increasingly difficult battles. And in the utilitarianism that so effectively inhibits idealism, they will not find an inspiration powerful enough to maintain cohesion. An illustrious thinker who compared the slave of ancient societies to a particle undigested by the social system might use a similar comparison to characterize the situation of the strong Germanic strain now identifiable in the Mid- and Far West. There, preserved intact—in temperament, social organization, and customs—are all the traits of a German nature that in many of its most profound and most vigorous specificities must be considered to be antithetical to the American character. In addition, a civilization destined to endure and expand in the world, a civilization that has not, in the manner of an Oriental empire, become mummified, or lost its aptitude for variety, cannot indefinitely channel its energies and ideas in one, and only one, direction. Let us hope that the spirit of that titanic society, which has until today been characterized solely by *Will* and *Utility*, may one day be known for its intelligence, sentiment, and idealism. Let us hope that from that enormous crucible will ultimately emerge the exemplary human being, generous, balanced, and select, whom Spencer, in a work I have previously cited, predicted would be the product of the costly work of the melting pot. But let us not expect to find such a person either in the present reality of that nation or in its immediate evolution. And let us refuse to see an exemplary civilization where there exists only a clumsy, though huge, working model that must still pass through many corrective revisions before it acquires the serenity and confidence with which a nation that has achieved its perfection crowns its work—the powerful ascent that Leconte de Lisle describes in "Le sommeil du condor" [The Dream of the Condor] as an ascent that ends in Olympian tranquillity.

very great nation should be seen by posterity, by history, as a tree whose harmonious growth has produced a fruit whose purified nectar offers to the future the idealism of its fragrance and the fecundity of its seed. Without this lasting *human* result upheld above the transitory ends of the *useful,* the power and grandeur of empires are but a night's dream in the existence of humankind, for, like the visions in our dreams, they do not deserve to be woven into the cloth of events that issues from the great loom of life.

Great civilizations, great nations, in the historical sense, are those that, once their time has passed, leave vibrating throughout eternity the harmony of their spirit and imprint their heritage upon posterity—as Carlyle said of his heroes—like a new and divine proportion in the sum of things. In Goethe's *Faust,* when Helena, called from the realm of night, again descends into the shades of Hades, she leaves Faust her tunic and her veil. These vestments are not the goddess herself but, as she has worn them, they are imbued with her supreme divinity and have the virtue of elevating whoever possesses them above all vulgarity.

A fully defined society that limits its idea of civilization to accumulating wealth, and its idea of justice to distributing that wealth equitably among its members, will find that its cities are, essentially, no different from anthills or beehives. Populous, magnificent, opulent cities are not sufficient proof of the constancy and intensity of a civilization. The large city is, no one would deny it, a necessary organism of high culture. It is the natural ambience of the highest manifestation of the spirit. It was with good reason that Edgard Quinet said, "The soul that comes to draw its strength and energy from an intimate communication with humankind, that soul, which is man in his greatness, cannot be formed, or grow, amid the petty interests of a small city." The quantitative greatness of a nation, however, as well as the material grandeur of its instruments, its weapons, its dwellings, are only the *milieus* of a civilization's identity, and never the effects in which that civilization endures. Of the stones that composed Carthage, not one particle survives that is transfigured into spirit and light. The enormity of Babylon and Nineveh do not in human mercy fill even the hollow of a hand when compared to the hallowed space that stretches from Athens to Piraeus. In an ideal perspective, a city cannot be considered large solely because it occupies a space as vast as the area surrounding Nimrod's Tower of Babel. Nor is it strong solely because it is capable of raising about itself Babylonian walls wide enough for six chariots abreast. Nor is it beautiful solely because, as in Babylon, alabaster shines from the parapets of its palaces, and it is garlanded with the gardens of Queen Semiramis.

In this ideal perspective, a city is great when its spiritual environs surpass the soaring peaks and depths of the seas, and when the sound of its name illuminates for posterity an entire day of human history and an entire horizon of time. A city is strong and beautiful when its days are more than the unvarying repetition of a single echo circling and circling in an eternal spiral; when there is something in it that rises above the crowd; when among the lamps it lights by night is the vessel that accompanies the solitary wakefulness incited by thought, the vigil that incubates the idea that at the dawn is born as the cry that summons and the strength that leads human souls.

Only then can the physical growth and grandeur of the city measure the intensity of its civilization. Stately cities, proud clusters of houses, are less conducive to thought than the absolute silence of the desert—unless thought reigns over them. Reading Tennyson's "Maud," I came across a page that could well serve as a symbol for the torment of the spirit that is forced by society into solitude. Captive to anguishing delirium, the hero of the poem dreams that he is dead, buried a few feet beneath the pavement of a London street. Dead though he may be, consciousness still lingers in his lifeless body. The clamor and clatter of the street, rumbling and vibrating in his shallow grave, prohibit any dream of peace. The indifferent multitude weighs upon the mournful prison, and the hooves of the horses overhead beat into his brain with the seal of opprobrium. The days pass with inexorable slowness. The aspiration of the hero is to be buried deeper, "ever so little deeper," in the ground. The unintelligible hubbub serves merely to maintain in his sleepless consciousness the awareness of his imprisonment.

Our Latin America can already boast of cities whose physical grandeur and obvious cultivation will soon qualify them for inclusion among the first cities of the world. We do well to fear, however, that when serene thought draws near to rap upon their lavish exteriors—as upon a sealed bronze vase—no sound will be heard but the disconsolate ring of emptiness. We must similarly fear that cities whose names were once a symbol of glory in America—cities that knew a Mariano Moreno, a Bernardino Rivadavia, a Domingo Sarmiento, cities that took the lead in an immortal Revolution, cities that spread the names of their heroes and the words of their orators across a continent, like concentric ripples raised by a pebble cast upon tranquil waters—might end like Sidon, or Tyre, or Carthage.

It is your generation that must prevent this from happening; it is you, our youth, who must rise up, blood and muscle and nerve of the future. I want to see that generation personified in you. I speak to you now with the conviction that you are destined to lead others to battle on behalf of the spirit. The perseverance of your efforts must be joined deep within you to the certainty of triumph. Do not be faint-hearted in preaching the gospel of delicacy to the Scythians, the gospel of intelligence to the Boeotians, and the gospel of selflessness to the Phoenicians.

It is enough that thought insist on *being*—in demonstrating that it exists, as Diogenes proved of motion—for its dissemination to be inevitable and its triumph absolute.

Thought, through its own spontaneity, will gradually conquer all the space necessary to secure and consolidate its kingdom among the other manifestations of life. In the individual, through continuous activity, it will enhance and enlarge the size of the brain that houses it. Thinking races reveal in the increasing capacity of their crania the thrust of that internal activity. In society, thought will similarly enlarge the capacity of its sphere, without need for the intervention of any external force. But this persuasion, which should protect you from a discouragement whose only virtue is to eliminate the mediocre from the struggle, should also save you from impatiently and vainly exhorting time to alter its imperious pace.

Everything in our contemporary America that is devoted to the dissemination and defense of selfless spiritual idealism—art, science, morality, religious sincerity, a politics of ideas—must emphasize its unswerving faith in the future. The past belonged entirely to the arm that wages battle; the present, almost completely to the rugged arm that levels and constructs; the future—a future whose proximity is directly related to the degree of will and thought of those who desire it—offers both stability and ambience for the development of the best qualities of the soul.

Can you envision it, this America we dream of? Hospitable to the world of the spirit, which is not limited to the throngs that flock to seek shelter in her. Pensive, without lessening her aptitude for action. Serene and firm, in spite of her generous enthusiasms. Resplendent, with the charm of an incipient, calm purpose that recalls the expression on a child's face when the germ of a troubled thought begins to disturb its captivating grace. Hold this America in your thoughts. The honor of your future history depends on your having constantly before the eyes of your soul the vision of this regenerated America, filtered down from above upon the realities of the present, like the sun's rays that penetrate the vast rose window of a Gothic nave to cast their warm glow upon somber walls. If you are not to be the founders, you will be the immediate precursors. Future rolls of glory will laud the memory of precursors. Edgard Quinet, a profound student of history and nature, observed that a new human type, a new social unity, a new personification of civilization, is often preceded by a dispersed and still undeveloped group whose role is analogous in the life of societies to that of the *prophetic species* Oswald Heer proposed for biological evolution. The new type begins by representing small degrees of individual and isolated deviations. With time these individualities are organized into a "variety"; then that "variety" finds a medium favorable to its propagation and perhaps ascends to the rank of a specific species. Finally, let us say it in the words of Quinet, *"the group becomes a crowd, and rules."*

This is why in work and battle your moral philosophy must be the reverse of the Horatian *carpe diem,* a philosophy that does not pertain to the present except as a step to offer a firm footing, or as a breach through which enemy walls may be penetrated. You should not hope for a definitive victory in the immediate future, only that you obtain the optimum conditions for the battle. Your vigor and energy will find a powerful stimulus in this activity; there is the potential for great drama in playing the essentially active role of renovation and conquest and in refining the strengths of a heroically gifted generation, strengths which in Olympian serenity the golden ages of the spirit often bestow upon the acolytes of their glory. "It is not possessing good things," Taine wisely said, speaking of the glories of the Renaissance; ". . . it is not possessing good things, but attaining them, that gives men pleasure and a sense of power."

Perhaps it is a rash and ingenuous hope to believe that with a continuous and felicitous acceleration of evolution, with efficacious effort on your part, the period of one generation might suffice to transform the conditions of intellectual life in America from the early stages at which we now find ourselves to a level that would truly benefit society, to a truly dominant peak of achievement. But even when a total transformation is not within the realm of possibility, there can be progress. Even if you know that the first fruits of the soil you so laboriously worked were never to be served on your table, the work itself, if you are generous and strong, would be its own satisfaction. The most invigorating work is that which is realized without anticipation of immediate success. The most glorious effort is that which places hope just beyond the visible horizon. And the purest abnegation is that which denies in the present, not merely resounding applause and the reward of the laurel, but even the moral voluptuousness of satisfaction in a job well done.

There were in antiquity altars for the "unknown gods." I urge you to dedicate a part of your soul to the unknown future. As a society advances, concern about the future becomes a major factor in its evolution, an inspiration in its labors. From the confusion and lack of foresight of the savage, who can see into the future only as far as the hours remaining until sunset, and who has no concept that it is possible to have partial control over the days ahead, to our own thoughtful and prudent preoccupation with posterity, there is an enormous distance that some day may seem brief and insignificant. We are capable of progress only to the degree that we become capable of adapting our acts to conditions that are increasingly distant from us in space and time. The certainty that we are contributing to work that will survive us, work that will benefit the future, enhances our sense of human dignity, helping us to triumph over the limitations of our nature. If, through some calamity, humanity were to despair of the immortality of the individual consciousness, the most religious sentiment that could replace it would be the one born from the belief that even after the dissolution of the soul, the best of what it has felt and dreamed—its most personal, its purest, essence—will persist in the heritage transmitted by generations of human beings, in the same way that the shining ray of a dead star lives on in infinity to touch us with its tender and melancholy light.

In the life of human societies, the future is a perfect equivalence of visionary thought. From the pious veneration of the past and the cult of tradition, on the one hand, and, on the other, from bold movement toward what is to come, is composed the noble strength that in raising the collective spirit above the limitations of the present communicates the sentiments and agitations of a society. Men and nations, in the opinion of Fouillée, work under the inspiration of ideas, while irrational beings react to the stimulus of the instincts. According to that same thinker, the society that struggles and labors, often unknowingly, to make an idea reality is imitating the instinctive work of a bird that, as it constructs its nest, obsessed by an imperious internal image, is obeying both an unconscious memory of the past and a mysterious presentiment of the future.

In eliminating self-interest, thought inspired in a concern for destinies beyond our own purifies, soothes, and ennobles. Our century is to be honored for the fact that the compelling strength of this concern for the future, and for the dignity of the rational being, was manifest so clearly in it. For even in the midst of the most absolute pessimism, even in the midst of the bitter philosophy of dissolution and nothingness borne to Western civilization from the East on the petals of the lotus flower, Karl von Hartmann has predicated, with obvious logic, man's austere obligation to continue the work of perfection, of working for the future, so that as the process of evolution is hastened, the final end will be more quickly attained—the end of all sorrow, and all life.

[97]

It is not in the name of death, as Hartmann would have it, but in the name of life itself, and hope, that I call upon you to dedicate a portion of your soul to the work of the future. In making this plea, I have taken my inspiration from the gentle and serene image of my Ariel. The beneficent spirit that Shakespeare—perhaps with the divine unawareness frequent in inspired intuitions—imbued with such high symbolism is clearly represented in the statue, his ideals magnificently translated by art into line and contour. Ariel is reason and noble sentiment. Ariel is the sublime instinct for perfectibility, by virtue of which human clay—the *miserable clay* of which Arimanes' spirits spoke to Manfred—is exalted and converted into a creature that lives in the glow of Ariel's light: the center of the universe. Ariel is for Nature the crowning achievement of her labors, the last figure in the ascending chain, the spiritual flame. A triumphant Ariel signifies idealism and order in life; noble inspiration in thought; selflessness in morality; good taste in art; heroism in action; delicacy in customs. He is the eponymous hero in the epic of the species. He is the immortal protagonist: his presence inspired the earliest feeble efforts of rationalism in the first prehistoric man when for the first time he bowed his dark brow to chip at rock or trace a crude image on the bones of the reindeer; his wings fanned the sacred bonfire that the primitive Aryan, progenitor of civilized peoples, friend of light, ignited in the mysterious jungles of the Ganges in order to forge with his divine fire the scepter of human majesty. In the later evolution of superior races, Ariel's dazzling light shines above souls that have surpassed the natural limits of humankind, above heroes of thought and fantasy, as well as those of action and sacrifice, above Plato on the promontory of Sunium, as well as above St. Francis of Assisi in the solitude of Monte della Verna. Ariel's irresistible strength is fueled by the ascendant movement of life. Conquered a thousand times over by the indomitable rebellion of Caliban, inhibited by victorious barbarism, asphyxiated in the smoke of battles, his transparent wings stained by contact with the "eternal dunghill of Job," Ariel rebounds, immortal; Ariel recovers his youth and beauty and responds with agility to Prospero's call, to the call of all those who love him and invoke him in reality. At times his beneficent empire reaches even those who deny him and ignore him. He often directs the blind forces of evil and barbarism so that, like others, they will contribute to the work of good. Ariel will pass through human history, humming, as in Shakespeare's drama, his melodious song to animate those who labor and those who struggle, until the fulfillment of the unknown plan permits him—in the same way that in the drama he is liberated from Prospero's service—to break his material bonds and return forever to the center of his divine fire.

I want you to remember my words, but even more, I beseech you to cherish the indelible memory of my statue of Ariel. I want the airy and graceful image of this bronze to be imprinted forever in the innermost recesses of your mind. I remember that once while enjoying a coin collection in a museum my attention was captured by the legend on an ancient coin: the word *Hope*, nearly effaced from the faded gold. As I gazed at that worn inscription, I pondered what its influence might have been. Who knows what noble and active role in forming the character and affecting the lives of human generations we could attribute to that simple theme's working its insistent suggestion upon those who held it in their hands? Who knows, as it circulated from hand to hand, how much fading joy was renewed, how many generous plans brought to fruition, how many evil proposals thwarted, when men's gaze fell upon the inspiring word incised, like a graphic cry, on the metallic disc. May this image of Ariel—imprinted upon your hearts—play the same imperceptible but decisive role in your own lives. In darkest hours of discouragement, may it revive in your consciousness an enthusiasm for the wavering ideal and restore to your heart the ardor of lost hope. Once affirmed in the bastion of your inner being, Ariel will go forth in the conquest of souls. I see him, far in the future, smiling upon you with gratitude from above as your spirit fades into the shadows. I have faith in your will, in your strength, even as I have faith in the will and strength of those to whom you will give life, to whom you will transmit your work. Often I am transported by the dream that one day may be a reality: that the Andes, soaring high above our America, may be carved to form the pedestal for this statue, the immutable altar for its veneration.

hese were the words of Prospero. After pressing the master's hand with filial affection, the youthful disciples drifted away. His gently spoken words, like the lament of ringing crystal, lingered in the air. It was the last hour of the day. A ray from the dying sun penetrated the room, pierced the shadows, and fell upon the bronze brow of the statue, seeming to strike a restless spark of life in Ariel's exalted eyes. Lingering in the gloom, the beam of light suggested the gaze the spirit, captive in the bronze, cast upon the departing youths. They left in silent unanimity, each absorbed in serious thought—the delicate distillation of meditation that a saint exquisitely compared to the slow and gentle fall of dewdrops upon the fleece of a lamb. When their harsh encounter with the throng brought them back to the surrounding reality, it was night. A warm, serene summer night. The grace and quietude the night spilled upon the earth from its ebony urn triumphed over the rudeness of man's accomplishments. Only the presence of the multitude forbade ecstasy.

A warm breeze rippled the evening air with languid and delicious abandon, like wine trembling in the goblet of a bacchant. The shadows cast no darkness on the pure night sky, but painted its blue with a shade that seemed to reflect a pensive serenity. In that cobalt sky, great stars sparkled amid an infinite retinue: Aldebaran, girded with purple; Sirius, like the cup of a nielloed silver calyx upturned above the world; the Southern Cross, whose open arms extend across our America as if in defense of one last hope . . .

It was then, following the prolonged silence, that the youngest of the group, the one they called "Enjolras" on account of his resemblance to Hugo's pensive character, pointed to the meandering human flock, and then to the radiant beauty of the night:

"As I watch the passing throng, I notice that although people are not gazing at the sky, the sky is gazing at them. Something is descending from above upon these indifferent masses, dark as newly turned earth. The scintillation of the stars is like the movement of the sower's hands."

Reader's Reference

Adorno, Theodor Wiesengrund (1903–1969). German philosopher influential in the German intellectual revival that followed World War II. Also a student of sociology, psychology, and musicology.

Alberdi, Juan Bautista (1810–1884). Prominent among nineteenth-century Argentine political thinkers. A proponent of centralization of government; also largely responsible for massive European immigration during that century.

Atomism. The philosophy that proposes discrete, irreducible elements. Propounded in the fifth century B.C.; revived under influence of Arabic philosophers in Middle ages, and in the seventeenth century by Pierre Gassendi.

Augustine, Saint (354–430). Doctor of the church, his writings are the basis for great polemics on the question of grace and predestination. Many scholars consider him to be the father of theology.

Bagehot, Walter (1826–1877). English economist, political analyst, and influential journalist. He has been described as "England's most versatile genius." The quotations on pp. 53 and 71 are from his *Physics and Politics,* rev. ed. (London and New York: Colonial Press, 1900).

Bakhtin, Mikhail Mikhailovich (1895–1975). Russian critic, literary and language theorist. Forced for political reasons to withdraw from active literary life, he worked in relative obscurity until "discovered" by young Russian literary scholars.

Barnes, Leonard (1895–19??). Journalist, South African agriculturist, author, adviser to the United Nations and British government on African affairs; author of numerous works on Africa and Empire.

Bartholdi, Fréderic-Auguste (1834–1904). French sculptor of the Statue of Liberty.

Baudelaire, Charles (1821–1867). Poet and critic, one of the great figures of French literature. Often considered the first modern; also known for his translations of Edgar Allan Poe.

Bérenger, Victor Henry (1867–1952). French essayist whose *L'aristocratie intellectuelle* (1895) greatly influenced Rodó's thinking.

Boethius (480–524). Translator of Aristotle, Boethius was a link between classical texts and medieval scholars.

Borges, Jorge Luis (1899–1986). One of the principal figures of twentieth-century literature; Argentine poet and short story writer. For his brief prose pieces he coined the term "fiction."

Bourget, Paul (1852–1935). French critic and author influenced by Hippolyte Taine (*q.v.*). His novel *Le disciple,* however, refutes the Taine position, urging a return to traditional morality.

Breton, André (1896–1966). French critic, essayist, and poet, best known for his leading role in the Surrealist movement.

Buñuel, Luis (1900–1983). Spanish experimental filmmaker: *Un chien andalou* (1928), *Viridiana* (1961), and *Tristana* (1970).

Campanella, Tommaso (1568–1638). Italian Platonic philosopher and writer arrested for heresy in 1599. His most famous work is *La Città del Sole* (1602).

Carlyle, Thomas (1795–1881). Victorian English essayist and historian. Author of *The French Revolution* (1837).

Channing, William Ellery (1780–1842). A Unitarian clergyman, abolitionist, and leading figure in the growth of New England's Transcendentalism.

Chasles, Philarète (1798–1873). French scholar. The director of the Mazarine Library and professor of the Collège de France, he was the foremost specialist of his time on European literatures.

Chateaubriand, François-August Réné (1768–1848). French author of the Romantic period whose exotic accounts of America and American Indians greatly influenced European perceptions.

Chénier, André (1762–1794). Considered by some critics to be the greatest of eighteenth-century French poets. He was the inspiration for one of Chateaubriand's principal works, *Génie du christianisme* (1802).

Chevalier, Michel (1806–1879). A French economist who advocated industrial development as a key to social progress.

Cicero, Marcus Tullius (106–43 B.C.). Famous for being Rome's greatest orator; also a philosopher and statesman strongly opposed to Caesar's dictatorship.

Cleanthes (331?–231? B.C.). Successor to Zeno as leader of the Stoic (*v.* Stoicism) school, to whose teachings he brought a religious zeal.

Comte, Auguste (1798–1858). French writer, the founder of Positivism (q.v.), a philosophy he expounded in *Cours de philosophie positive* (1830–1842).

Darío, Rubén (pseudonym of Félix Rubén García Sarmiento, 1867–1916). One of the foremost poets of the Spanish language and leader of the South American literary movement known as *modernismo.*

Daudet, Alphonse (1848–1897). French humorist, short story writer, and novelist who portrayed life in Paris and the southern provinces.

Deschamps, Gaston (1861–1931). French critic, journalist, and student of politics. He replaced Anatole France as the literary critic of *Le Temps.*

Dickinson, Emily (1836–1886). North American poet who, although she published only seven poems during her lifetime, is considered one of the country's greatest; best known for her brief lyrics.

Dynamism. A philosophical system that explains the universe in terms of force or energy.

Elgar, Sir Edward William (1857–1934). English composer influenced by German Romanticism and considered responsible for a renaissance in English music.

Emerson, Ralph Waldo (1803–1882). Poet and essayist. A New England Transcendentalist and member of the Concord group, which included Thoreau and Hawthorne (*q.v.*)

Erasmus, Desiderius (1466–1536). Dutch humanist thought to be one of the greatest classical scholars of the Renaissance. An ordained Augustinian (*v.* Saint Augustine), he was a contemporary and friend of Sir Thomas More (*q.v.*).

Faust. A historical character who died in 1540, Faust, or Faustus, is known as a legendary German magician who sold his soul to the devil in return for knowledge and power.

Flaubert, Gustave (1821–1880). Considered to be among the foremost novelists of French Realism. Probably his best-known work is *Madame Bovary* (1857), a classic depiction of bourgeois life.

Fouillée, Alfred (1838–1912). French thinker who, along with Renan (*q.v.*), deeply influenced the writing of Rodó—particularly his *L'idée moderne du droit en Allemagne, en Angleterre et en France* (1878).

Fox, Charles James (1747–1806). English politician, abolitionist, writer, and supporter of the French Revolution; the first foreign secretary in English history.

France, Anatole (pseudonym of Anatole François Thibaut, 1844–1924). French author awarded the Nobel prize for literature in 1921; novelist, poet, and essayist.

Francia, José Gaspar Rodríguez (1766–1840). Paraguayan dictator known as "El Supremo." Francia cut off Paraguay from the rest of the world. He declared himself dictator in 1814, and ruled until his death.

Gogol, Nikolai Vasilyevich (1809–1952). A Russian novelist, short story writer, and dramatist; a forerunner of Russian Realism. Best-known work in English, "The Overcoat."

Guyau, Jean-Marie (1854–1888). French philosopher admired by Rodó. Principal work, *Esquisse d'une morale sans obligation ni sanction*.

Hamilton, Alexander (1755–1804). First U.S. secretary of the treasury; patriot, delegate to the Constitutional Convention, author (with James Madison and John Jay) of *The Federalist Papers*.

Hartmann, Karl Robert Eduard (1842–1906). German philosopher called the philosopher of the Unconscious (the inexplicable forces of nature). His system combined Schopenhauer's pessimism and Hegel's optimism in regard to the future of mankind.

Hawthorne, Nathaniel (1804–1864). Short story writer and novelist and one of the masters of North American literature. With his haunting tales, Hawthorne helped establish the North American short story as a significant art form.

Heer, Osvald (1809–1883). Swiss paleontologist and professor of the Polytechnicum de Zurich. Major work is probably *Die Urwelt der Schweitz* (1865), translated into English in 1876 as *The*

Primaeval World of Switzerland.

Hegel, Georg Wilhelm Friedrich (1770–1831). German Idealist philosopher, originator of a dialectical system that directly influenced Existentialism, Marxism, and Positivism (*q.v.*).

Helvetius, Claude-Adrien (1715–1771). A French philosopher, one of the Encyclopedists. He believed that all men are equally capable of learning.

Horace (Quintus Horatius Flaccus, 65–8 B.C.). Under Augustus, Latin lyric poet and satirist. Best known for his *Satires, Odes,* and *Epistles.*

Hugo, Victor (1802–1885). A towering figure among French Romanticists; poet, dramatist, and novelist. Principal prose works: *Les Misérables* (1862) and *Les travailleurs de la mer* (1866).

Huysmans, Joris-Karl (1848–1907). French novelist who reflects France's post–World War I pessimism. *A rebours* (1884) has been described as "the breviary of decadence."

Ibsen, Henrik (1828–1906). Norwegian dramatist, one of the leading figures of modern realist drama. Particularly effective in his depiction of nineteenth-century women in conflict with their traditional roles. The quotation on p. 64 is from his *Complete Major Prose Plays,* trans. Rolf Fjelde (New York: New American Library, 1978).

James, Henry (1843–1916). North American master of the psychological novel. His distinctive prose style may be best illustrated in *The Wings of the Dove* (1902) and *The Golden Bowl* (1904).

Kant, Immanuel (1724–1804). German philosopher. A leading figure of the Enlightenment and foremost among philosophers of all time. His *Critique of Pure Reason* (1781) and *Critique of Practical Reason* (1788) stand as a basis for Kantianism and Idealism.

Kipling, Rudyard (1865–1936). English author born in Bombay, usually remembered in connection with his tales and poems of British colonial soldiers in India and Burma. He received the Nobel prize for literature in 1907.

Konrad, George (Gyoergy Konrad, 1933–). Hungarian novelist and social worker. Konrad was a childhood victim of the Nazi occupation.

Laboylaye, Edouard Réné Lefebvre (1811–1883). French historian and political figure; administrator of the Collège de France.

Among his works, *Paris en Amérique* (1863).

Lastarria, José Victoriano (1817–1888). Chilean essayist, jurist, journalist prominent in national and continental growth of literature and nationalism.

Lavoisier, Antoine Laurent (1743–1794). French scientist considered to be the father of modern chemistry. He explained combustion and described the role of oxygen in respiration. Also active in improving social and economic conditions in France.

Leconte de Lisle, Charles-Marie-René (1818–1894). French poet whose *Poésies barbares* established him as leader of the Parnassians. His influence diminished, however, with the rise of Baudelaire and the Symbolists.

Lemaître, Jules (1853–1914). French critic, dramatist, lecturer, biographer; his critical stance reflects the contemporary reaction against "scientific" criticism.

Longfellow, Henry Wadsworth (1817–1882). Nineteenth-century North America's most popular poet, Longfellow created a new body of Romantic American legends. Among his best known works: *The Song of Hiawatha* (1855) and *The Courtship of Miles Standish* (1863).

Macaulay, Thomas Babington (1800–1859). English historian whose greatest work was his five-volume *History of England* (1849–1861), left unfinished at his death. His work has been praised for narrative style but criticized for subjectivity.

Malesherbes, Chrétien Guillaume de Lamoignon de (1721–1794). French legal expert who tried to initiate political reforms during the reigns of Louis XV and Louis XVI. He defended the king before the convention, however, and was guillotined as a counter-revolutionary.

Marden, Orison Swett (1848–1924). North American booster whose *Pushing to the Front* offended Rodó. The book was widely translated and is easily available in Spanish today.

Martha, Benjamin-Constant (1820–1895). French professor and writer. A member of the Academy of Moral and Political Sciences; his books focused on questions of morality.

Maud. A monodrama published in 1855 by A. Lord Tennyson containing some of his best love lyrics.

Medici family. Italian dynasty of rulers of Florence, and later

Tuscany, from approximately 1434 to 1737. Famous for their patronage of the arts, as well as for political intrigue.

Melville, Herman (1819–1891). North American novelist universally acclaimed for his masterpiece, *Moby Dick* (1851), a philosophical inquiry into the nature of good and evil.

Michelet, Jules (1798–1874). French nationalist and Romantic historian, whose monumental *Histoire de France* appeared from 1833 to 1867. Like Macaulay, Michelet was praised for great dramatic power, but criticized for his subjective interpretation of the past.

Mill, John Stuart (1806–1873). Philosopher, political economist, proponent of Utilitarianism. His *A System of Logic* (1843), along with other major writings, contained most of the major tenets of nineteenth-century thought.

Mithradates VI (ca. 131–63 B.C.). Conqueror in 88 B.C. of the whole of Asia Minor, with the exception of a few cities, but was defeated in 85 B.C. by the Roman general Fimbria. He was eventually driven from power by Pompey.

Molière (pseudonym of Jean-Baptiste Poquelin, 1622–1673). French comic genius whose plays are among the greatest of world literature. He is particularly known for his caricatures of type, such as *Tartuffe* (1664), *Le misanthrope* (1666), and *Le bourgeois gentilhomme* (1670).

Monnier, Henri (1805–1877). French lithographer and caricaturist. His *Mémoires de Monsieur Joseph Prudhomme* (1857) created the legendary Prudhomme, an international symbol of mediocrity.

Montaigne, Michel (1533–1592). French writer, one of the great masters of the essay form. His three collections of *Essais* were tests of his opinions on a diversity of subjects.

Móntez, María (1920–1951). A native of the Dominican Republic. Móntez starred in countless Hollywood adventure films of the forties. She was known as the "Queen of Technicolor."

More, Sir Thomas (1477–1535). An English humanist and statesman known for his rejection of Henry VIII's right to lead the Church of England, a stand for which he was beheaded. Particularly relevant to the New World as author of *Utopia* (1515).

Moreno, Mariano (1778–1811). Argentine patriot and statesman, Moreno was the intellectual force behind Argentina's movement of independence. He was before his time in advocating complete separation from Spain.

Morice, Charles (1861–1918). French poet and critic, idealist and mystic. He collaborated in various literary reviews. His major work is *Littérature de tout à l'heure* (1889).

Napoleon (Bonaparte, 1769–1821). A legendary figure; French emperor of a large portion of Europe. A general in the French Revolution, Napoleon crowned himself emperor in 1804. In 1814 he was defeated and exiled to the island of Elba.

Nero (Lucius Domitius Ahenobarbus, or Nero Claudius Caesar, 37–68). The last of the Caesars, Nero was the fifth emperor of Rome and was noted for his cruelty.

Neruda, Pablo (pseudonym of Neftali Ricardo Reyes, 1904–1973). Chilean Nobel laureate. One of the most prolific and inventive of Spanish-language poets. Neruda was extremely influential in liberal politics and social causes.

Nietzsche, Friedrich (1844–1900). German philosopher, scholar, and social critic whose philosophical-sociological writings were a major influence on continental philosophy and literature. He hoped to create the "superman" who would rise above the "herd" of humanity.

Olmedo, José Joaquín (1780–1817). Ecuadorian poet and statesman. Best remembered for his "La victoria de Junín," which commemorates the victory of Simón Bolívar over Spanish forces.

Ortega y Gasset, José (1883–1955). Spanish philosopher, humanist, and critic. A member of the influential Generation of '98, he shared their preoccupation with the "problems" of Spain's political, economic, and cultural decline.

Pascal, Blaise (1623–1662). Religious philosopher, mathematician, physicist, founder of modern theory of probabilities. His ideas greatly influenced Rousseau, Bergson, and the Existentialists.

Plato (428–348 B.C.). One of the Greek philosophers who laid the foundations of Western culture. His philosophy is marked by a high regard for mathematics and its method by a spiritualistic view of life.

Poe, Edgar Allan (1809–1849). One of the most famous of North American poets and short story writers. Poe cultivated the macabre and excelled in the mystery story. Acknowledged today as one of the most original of American writers, his poetry was more highly valued in Europe than in his own country.

Positivism. A philosophical and ideological movement of the mid-nineteenth century, which argues that data are based on experience and that transcendent beliefs must be rejected. The writings of John Stuart Mill (*q.v.*) and Auguste Comte (*q.v.*) were central to this development.

Prudhomme. *See* Monnier.

Pythagoras (ca. 582–ca. 507 B.C.). Greek mathematician and philosopher who influenced the thinking of Plato and Aristotle. Although none of his writings have survived, he is usually credited with the theory of the function of numbers in mathematics and music.

Quinet, Edgar (1803–1875). French poet, historian, and political philosopher whose influence is most obvious in the reforms of the Third Republic. He advocated complete separation of church from political influence.

Renan, Joseph Ernest (1823–1892). French philosopher, scholar of religion. With Fouillée, the greatest influence on Rodó's thinking. He attributed the development of Christianity to popular imagination and was suspended from his educational post for referring to Jesus as an "incomparable man."

Rivadavia, Bernardino (1780–1845). First president of the Argentine Republic. He resisted British invasion of 1806 and supported independence from Spain. His administration was battered externally by war with Brazil, and internally in struggles with regional *caudillos*.

Rod, Edouard (1857–1910). Swiss critic and writer. A disciple of Zola, Rod later developed a personal style, the psychological novel. As a critic, he was a forerunner of comparative literature studies.

Rosas, Juan Manuel de (1793–1877). Symbol of Argentine political repression, Rosas was for seventeen years the dictator of Argentina. He was overthrown in 1852 and fled to exile in England.

Rosenkrantz, Karl (1805–1879). German philosopher, literary historian, critic. Although a disciple of Hegel, Rosenkrantz developed his own points of view, positing absolute idealism as the most perfect form of idealism.

Rousseau, Jean-Jacques (1712–1778). Swiss-French philosopher, political theorist, author, and composer. Rousseau had great faith in the existence of the common good and rightness of the general will. He greatly influenced the French Revolution and leaders of literary Romanticism.

Saint-Victor, Paul de (1825–1881). French literary critic noted for articles on theater. Author of *Hommes et dieux* (1867).

Santa Anna, Antonio López de (1794–1876). Mexican general, four times president of Mexico, three times exiled. Famous for his victory at the Alamo, but also for the major loss of Mexican territory to the United States.

Sarmiento, Domingo Faustino (1811–1888). Argentine editor, statesman, writer; Argentina's first civilian president. Sarmiento was a strong proponent of public education. His *Facundo, o la civilización y la barbarie* (1845) is one of the landmark sociological works of Latin American literature.

Schiller, Friedrich von (1759–1805). German poet, dramatist, and literary theorist. His friendship with Goethe was one of the richest in literary history, and his importance in modern German literature is second only to Goethe's.

Scholasticism. Philosophy originated among Medieval scholars, called *doctores scholastici*. A comprehensive system of interpreting all the materials of Greek and Roman classicism through a Christian point of view.

Seneca, Lucius Annaeus (The Younger, 4 B.C.–A.D. 65). Philosopher, statesman, orator, Rome's leading intellectual of first century A.D.—the first phase of Nero's reign.

Shakespeare, William (1564–1616). Arguably, the greatest writer of all time. *The Tempest* (1611) provided Rodó with the figures of the magus Prospero, the airy sprite Ariel, and the monster Caliban.

Solon (ca. 638–ca. 559 B.C.). Athenian poet, statesman, reformer, and legislator who ended exclusive aristocratic control of government, thus eliminating serfdom.

Spencer, Herbert (1820–1903). English philosopher and early evolutionist who believed in a progression from the simple to the complex. He proposed a system based on a synthesis of scientific investigation and bio- and sociological phenomena.

Stoicism. Greco-Roman school of philosophy founded by Zeno and based on premise that virtue is the only good. The system stresses duty and holds that the universe is fundamentally rational.

Taine, Hippolyte (1828–1893). French critic and historian, one of the prime exponents of French Positivism (*q.v.*). He hoped to explain literature and history through the triple influence of race, environment, and epoch.

Tarde, Gabriel (1813–1904). Sociologist, criminologist, and versatile social scientist. He originated a social formula based on a distinction between inventive and imitative persons.

Thackeray, William Makepeace (1811–1863). Victorian English novelist and satirist whose reputation rests largely on *Vanity Fair* (published serially in 1847–1848), a satirical novel of nineteenth-century manners.

Thomism. Philosophy and theological system devised by Thomas Aquinas. He distinguished between essence and existence and argued that the soul is unique. His writing is generally recognized as among the greatest works on human thought.

Tocqueville, Alexis de (1805–1859). French political scientist and historian; a liberal whose greatest commitment was to human freedom. His *De la démocracie en Amérique* (1835) is one of the earliest and most perceptive studies of the American political system.

Uhland, Johann Ludwig (1787–1862). German poet, lawyer, and professor prominent in Medieval studies. Active in politics. German nationalism inspired much of Uhland's poetry.

Vallejo, César (1895–1938). Peruvian poet identified with suffering of the underclasses. Much of his writing was done in Paris in self-imposed exile. He became a Marxist and defended the Republican cause in the Spanish Civil War.

Annotated Bibliography

EDITIONS OF *ARIEL*

This chronological listing was compiled from the combined resources listed under References and the holdings of the University of Missouri, Columbia, Library.

Ariel [with *La vida nueva*]. Montevideo: Impr. de Dornaleche y Reyes, 1900.

Ariel [with *La vida nueva*], second edition. Prologue by Leopoldo Alas (Clarín). Montevideo: Impr. de Dornaleche y Reyes, 1900. Alas's prologue introduced *Ariel* to a public that did not as yet know the book. He describes Rodó as "one of the most notable young critics of Latin America" and reports that Rodó exhorts his readers not to allow themselves to be seduced by the siren of the North, but "to be . . . always what they are . . . that is, *Spanish,* sons of Classicism and Christianity." This basic edition appears in a number of countries, with various publishers. The most widely disseminated of any edition. Basic Rodó library.

Ariel. Supplement to *Revista Literaria* (Santo Domingo, 1901). Incomplete. According to Víctor Pérez Petit, an unauthorized version, but proudly reported by Jaime Julio as being the first publication of the work outside Uruguay.

Ariel. Published serially in *Cuba Literaria,* nos. 29–44 (Havana, January–April, 1905). Authorized; published by Max Henríquez Ureña.

Ariel. Monterrey: n.p., 1908. Sponsored by Porfirio G. González, governor of the state of Nuevo León.

Ariel. Mexico City: Escuela Nacional Preparatoria de México, 1908.

Both Arturo Scarone and Emir Rodríguez Monegal question this date.

Ariel. Monterrey: Lozano, 1908.

Only Thomas L. Welch lists this edition.

Ariel. Prologue by Leopoldo Alas [Clarín]. Valencia: F. Sempere y Cía, n.d.

Clemente Pereda lists two editions, 1908 and 1910.

Also contains "Liberalismo y Jacobinismo" and "La transformación personal en la creación artística." The 1910 Serrano edition lists *previous* editions, attributing a 1908 date of publication to this volume. A copy examined at the University of Missouri, Columbia, bears the hand-written notation, "Montevideo, 3 julio, 1911." This is the fourteenth entry in the Rodríguez Monegal *Obras completas* bibliography. It is the first entry in Welch— with an unattributed date.

Ariel. Montevideo: Impr. Henrich y Cía., 1910.

Published by José María Serrano for the Librería Cervantes.

Ariel. Montevideo: Impr. Henrich y Cía., 1911.

Like the 1910 edition, published by José María Serrano.

Ariel. Valencia: F. Sempere, 1911.

Listed only by Pereda.

Ariel. Madrid: Editorial América, 1915.

Published as part of *Cinco ensayos.* Listed only by Pereda.

Ariel. Madrid: Biblioteca Nueva, 1917.

Published as part of *Páginas escogidas.* Listed only by Pereda.

Ariel. Madrid: Editorial América, 1918.

Published as part of *Cinco ensayos.* Listed only by Pereda.

Ariel. Madrid: Editorial Lux, 1918.

Only Welch lists this edition.

Ariel. Prologue by Leopoldo Alas. Madrid: n.p., 1919.

Neither Rodríguez Monegal nor Scarone lists a publisher. Pereda calls it an "unlawful edition."

Ariel. Prologue by Leopoldo Alas. Montevideo: n.p., 1920.

A copy examined in the University of Missouri, Columbia, library is paperbound. The four-color cover illustration depicts a winged Ariel ascending toward the sun.

Ariel. Valencia: Editorial Cervantes, 1920.

Title page is headed, "Brevario de la juventud."

Ariel. Barcelona: Editorial Radium, 1922.

Pereda lists publisher as "Radiu."

Ariel. Translated, with an introductory essay by F. J. Stimson. Boston: Houghton Mifflin, 1922.

Stimson, in his introduction, recalls the return in 1921 of Rodó's remains to his native Montevideo. Realizing that Rodó "is still little known in North America," Stimson considers it a "grateful task . . . to essay the translation" of what he considers Rodó's finest book. One sees the labor of love in this work. Stimson was the former U.S. ambassador to Argentina and neither a career translator nor a student of language. The errors of understanding in the translation derive from the latter fact. The often inspired, seemingly intuitive moments evolve from his obvious sympathy for the text.

Ariel. Prologue by Leopoldo Alas. Valencia: Sociedad Editorial Prometeo, n.d.

Also contains "Liberalismo y Jacobinismo" and "La transformación en la creación artística." Scarone notes that the same *editorial* published two additional versions; none of the three is dated.

Ariel. Liberalismo y Jacobinismo. Prologue by Rafael Altamira. Barcelona: Editorial Cervantes, 1926.

Altamira comments very briefly on the "continuing success of *Ariel.*" He finds Rodó to be "head and shoulders" above most "modern" writers. Since Rodó's ideas are applicable in the "mother country," Altamira believes it is as important for Spanish youth to read *Ariel* as for those of America. A copy of the Altamira edition examined in the University of Missouri, Columbia, Library is the fourth printing, dated 1930, confirming at least that number of editions.

Ariel. Edited and with introduction, notes, and vocabulary by Alberto Nin Frías and John D. Fitz-Gerald. Chicago: B. H. Sanborn, 1928.

Ariel. Edited and with an introduction by William F. Rice. Chicago: University of Chicago Press, 1929.

Ariel. Translation into Portuguese by Hermes da Fonseca. Rio de Janeiro: Renascença, 1933.

Ariel. Montevideo: Claudio García, 1935.

Ariel. Prologue by Rafael Altamira. Santiago: Ercilla, 1935.

Ariel. Montevideo: G. García, 1939.

Sponsored by Biblioteca Rodó de Literatura e Historia. Welch also lists a third edition in 1941, a fourth in 1943, and a fifth in 1944.

Ariel. Prologue by Mario de la Cueva. Mexico City: Universidad Nacional Autónoma, 1942.

Ariel. Prologue by Leopoldo Alas. Buenos Aires: Editorial Sopena, 1944.

Welch lists this entry, out of chronology, as a second edition.

Ariel. Motivos de Proteo (selection). Buenos Aires: W. M. Jackson, 1945. [Second edition, 1946]

Ariel. Prologue by Juan Carlos Gómez Haedo. Montevideo: Colombino, 1947.

Handsomely produced, large-type edition with original illustrations by Antonio Peña. Gómez Haedo suggests that Rodó should not be criticized for ignoring class struggles, that it was not his intent to create a social structure. He reviews Rodó's life and influences. He argues that Rodó's dream of "beauty, poetry, art, good" is not dead and that democracy finally "will resolve into harmony with the highest and purest ideals of the human soul." The copy in the University of Missouri, Columbia, Library is 161 pages. Welch lists another edition, same year, of 123 pages.

Ariel. Buenos Aires: Editorial Tor, 1947.

Ariel y cuatro estudios críticos sobre J. E. Rodó. Buenos Aires: D. A. Espino, 1947.

Studies are by Clarín, Rubén Darío, Unamuno, and Gómez Restrepo.

Ariel. Prologue by Leopoldo Alas, Mexico City: Espasa-Calpe Mexicana, 1948.

My paperback copy is designated as the "second edition, 1961." (Welch also lists a third edition in 1963.) Rodríguez Monegal lists an Espasa-Calpe Buenos Aires edition, which is undoubtedly identical.

Ariel. Mexico City: Editorial Navaro-Mexico, 1957.

Ariel. Selection, prologue, and notes by José Pereira Rodríguez. Buenos Aires: Editorial Kapelusz, 1962.

Also listed in 1966, plus a "second edition" in 1971.

Ariel. Liberalismo y Jacobinismo. Prologue by José Pereira Rodríguez. Montevideo: Biblioteca Artigas, 1964.

Contains updated biographical information based on William J. Berrien's dissertation. Pereira examines *Ariel's* lasting virtues. Although the world has greatly changed, he finds that Prospero's lesson has withstood "human inconstancy." Pereira adds that this Prologue was included in an edition (undated) published by the Editorial Kapeluz (*sic*), with the authorization of the Ministerio de Instrucción Pública y Previsión Social.

Ariel. Mexico City: Editora Nacional, 1966.

Ariel. Liberalismo y Jacobinismo. Buenos Aires: Ediciones Depalma, 1967.

Ariel. Edited and with prologue by Gordon Brotherston. Cambridge: Cambridge University Press, 1967.

Excellent introduction. Brotherston believes that Fouillée is more influential in *Ariel* than the more often acknowledged Renan and Shakespeare. His even-handed essay examines the flaws and virtues of the work from the point of view of the contemporary reader. In conclusion, he encourages the reader "to confront afresh a work . . . still widely regarded as one of the fundamental works of Latin American literature." To prepare this edition, Brotherston returned to the text of the second edition of *Ariel*—proofread by a "meticulous" Rodó—and to Rodó's "preparatory materials" in the Rodó archives in Montevideo. Essential for Rodó library.

Ariel. Edited and with prologue by Alberto Zum Felde. Montevideo: Ediciones del Nuevo Mundo, 1967.

Zum Felde considers *Ariel* to be the "consecration of Latin American Modernism." At its publication it "achieved the greatest renown and significance in almost all Latin America . . . and the most representative expression of 'the general spiritual state' in all the countries of the Continent." Subsequent events, particularly those following the Second World War, have led to a diminution in its influence. However, "neither this change on the plane of historical reality, nor increased intellectual standards in North America, have essentially changed the order of cultural values." The Titan of the North is still there, with all its virtues and all its defects. Zum Felde's prologue encompasses Rodó's life and work as a whole. Excellent resource; excellent notes to text. Essential for Rodó library.

Ariel. Prologue by Leopoldo Alas. New York: Las Américas Publishing, 1967.

Ariel. Edited, with biographical note, introduction, and annotations by Edelmira González Maldonado. San Juan: Imprenta Estado Libre Asociado de Puerto Rico, 1968.

Ariel. Liberalismo y Jacobinismo. Ensayos: Rubén Darío, Bolívar, Montalvo. Edited and with prologue by Raimundo Lazo. Mexico City: Porrúa, 1970 [first edition, 1968].

Brief chronology and bibliography. Lazo's introduction discusses various interpretations of Rodó, the man; outlines the body of his work; refers to fluctuations in appreciation of his talents; relates him to the Modernist movement; and predicts what will endure of his writing. He classifies Rodó as elitist, a man who wishes to be a philosopher without ceasing to be an artist. Rodó's fusion of idealism and reality and his dual lesson of ethic and aesthetic will, in Lazo's opinion, endure. Welch lists a third edition in 1972, a fourth in 1977, and a fifth in 1979.

Ariel. Río Piedras: Editorial Edil, 1971.

Welch lists a second edition in 1979.

Ariel. Prologue by Leopoldo Alas. Montevideo: Editorial DOE, 1971.

Ariel. Ed. by Emilio Gascó Contell. Madrid: Editorial Anaya, 1971.

Ariel. Lima: Editorial Peisa, 1971.

Ariel. Prologue by Leopoldo Alas. Madrid: Espasa-Calpe, 1975. "Fifth edition."

Although there are previous entries for Espasa-Calpe México and Espasa-Calpe Argentina, this is the first mention of a Spanish publication.

Ariel. Motivos de Proteo. Prologue by Carlos Real de Azúa. Edited and with chronology by Angel Rama. Caracas: Biblioteca Ayacucho, 1976.

Superb chronology that sets events in Rodó's life against events in Uruguay, Latin America, and the "external world." Prologue reviews the ambience that produced Rodó; whether he was an original thinker or an adaptor of ideas; European literature of similar nature; the pendulum movement of attitudes and ideals; the history of editions of *Ariel;* and, especially, the breadth of critical reactions to the book's philosophy. In sum, Real de Azúa urges that Rodó be studied for the "great Latin American writer" that he is. Essential for Rodó library.

Ariel. Prologue by Adolfo Rodríguez Mallarini. Montevideo: Instituto Nacional del Libro, 1977.

Ariel (a fragment). Mexico City: Universidad Nacional Autónoma de México, 1978.

Ariel. Barcelona. Editorial Vasgos, 1979.

Obras selectas. Prologue by Arturo Marasso. Buenos Aires: El Ateneo, 1956.

A broad (851 pages) selection of Rodó's writings, including the complete text of *Ariel.* No notes or bibliography. Marasso compares the immediate success of *Ariel* to similar acceptance of Rubén Darío's *Azul.* He theorizes that Rodó did not intend in *Ariel* to "create an original system; his inspirations were those current in the philosophy of his century . . . but [he had no] fear of moving counter to it."

Obras completas. Seven volumes. Valencia/Barcelona: Editorial Cervantes, 1917–1927.

Contains *Motivos de Proteo* (Valencia, 1917); *El camino de Paros,* "Meditaciones y andanzas," miscellanea (Valencia, 1918); *El mirador de Próspero* (Valencia, 1919); *El que vendrá* and miscellanea (Barcelona, 1920); *Hombres de América,* "Montalvo," "Bolívar," "Rubén Darío," and selected political addresses (Barcelona, 1920); *Ariel. Liberalismo y Jacobinismo* (first edition, Valencia, 1920; second edition, Barcelona 1927; *see Editions*); and *Nuevos motivos de Proteo* (Barcelona, 1927). Basic Rodó library.

Obras completas de José Enrique Rodó. Official edition. Edited by José Pedro Segundo and Juan Antonio Zubillaga. Montevideo: Casa A. Barreiro Ramos, 1945–1958.

Volume 1 contains a 78-page introduction by Segundo pertaining primarily to the years 1895–1897; writing from *La Revista Nacional de Literatura y Ciencias Sociales;* poetry; and brief assessments from various critics. Volume 2 (1956), *El que vendrá; La novela nueva; Rubén Darío, Ariel, Liberalismo y Jacobinismo,* and assorted criticism. Volume 3 (1956) consists of *Motivos de*

Proteo. Volume 4 (1958), *El mirador de Próspero,* which is collected essays. The editors base the text of *Ariel* on the second edition, along with a close examination of the original manuscript. Most notes refer to problems of grammar or neologisms; occasional literary identifications. Basic Rodó library.

Obras completas de José Enrique Rodó. Buenos Aires: Ediciones Zamora, 1956 (first edition, 1948). Edited, compiled, and with a Prologue by Alberto José Vaccaro.

In his prologue Vaccaro places Rodó in the context of various literary figures, the literary movement *modernismo,* and the philosophical and literary currents of his time. Uncharacteristically, Vaccaro points out a number of flaws in Rodó's prose, which usually is highly praised. Of *Ariel,* the editor comments: "*Ariel* is outmoded insofar as its appraisal of the United States, now nullified by the cultural and scientific labors of the universities and research centers of that country, as well as by its Good Neighbor plan." In conclusion, Vaccaro describes Rodó as a "conscientious renovator of Spanish American criticism, an intellectual *sans* philosophical originality, and a painstaking stylist with grammatical weaknesses." Basically, this volume follows the selections of the Editorial Cervantes edition, with the addition of some twenty pages of speeches and articles (*Otros escritos*), *Nuevos motivos de Proteo* (*Los últimos motivos de Proteo*), and collected pieces from the *Revista Nacional de Literatura y Ciencias Sociales,* along with previously uncollected poems. Very few textual notes. Basic Rodó library.

Obras completas. Madrid: Aguilar, 1967 (first edition, 1957). Edited, and with introduction, prologue, and notes by Emir Rodríguez Monegal.

Rodríguez Monegal's preface outlines the problems and proposals of previous *Obras completas* (his is the fourth) and offers the rationale for this edition, in brief:

Works, respecting the bibliographic unities.

Posthumous Works, presented chronologically, and subdivided into ten sections, including substantial additions of letters, small pieces collected from newspapers and magazines, and unpublished materials.

Chronology and Bibliography.

Index of Proper Names. The second edition adds still more previously uncollected writings.

Rodríguez Monegal's introductory study of Rodó's "Life and Character" and his "Work" is fundamental. The photographs are a valuable contribution to an understanding of the man and the time. Of *Ariel* he writes, "It inaugurated a new American dimension of Modernism." He concludes that "none of his critics has been able [ultimately] to diminish Rodó's importance in the field of culture, his central position at the moment it was important to maintain the continuity of a tradition, and . . . to maintain a course." Seen in its totality [not only the Rodó of *Ariel* but also Rodó in the Chamber of Deputies], the balance of his work and his actions "continues to be favorable." There is very little editorial apparatus for text itself. This is by far the single most important book on Rodó. Essential for Rodó library.

WORKS ABOUT *ARIEL*
In English
*Works containing a significant bibliography.

Book

*Pereda, Clemente. *Rodó's Main Sources*. San Juan: Imprenta Venezuela, n.d.

An eclectic approach. Pereda deduces—from interviews with friends and family, a reconstruction of his library, and the works themselves—influences on Rodó's writing ranging from Greek and Roman times through nineteenth-century European, Latin American, and North American literatures. In Pereda's judgment, Rodó's most lasting work is to be found in his critical essays. Basic Rodó library.

Essays in Books

Crawford, William Rex. "A Reaction—Rodó." In *A Century of Latin-American Thought*. Rev. ed. Cambridge: Harvard University Press, 1961.

Crawford is widely quoted by North American students of

Rodó. He asks readers to draw their own conclusions in regard to the Arielist and anti-Arielist position. Rodó can be criticized for preoccupation with style, subservience to French masters, indifference to Indian culture, his obstinate optimism, his vagueness, and his lack of perception in regard to the United States. Crawford similarly questions whether Rodó "achieved that harmony between Hellenic paganism and Judaic Christianity that he (and Matthew Arnold) sought." His most successful attempt, says Crawford, "was his classic little book, *Ariel.*"

Davis, Harold Eugene. "José Enrique Rodó (1871–1917): *Ariel.*" In *Latin American Leaders*. New York: H. W. Wilson, 1949.

Davis considers Rodó to be the "most universal" of modern Latin American writers. He sees Rodó's essential weakness as his "dispassionate aloofness" and his contribution to American thought "still . . . a matter of profound difference of opinion." Of *Ariel* he says, "No other book by Rodó approaches *Ariel* in importance."

Franco, Jean. "The Select Minority: Arielismo and Criollismo, 1900–1918." In *The Modern Culture of Latin American Society and the Artist*. Rev. ed. Middlesex: Pelican, 1970.

Franco writes that "*Ariel*'s enormous popularity arose from the fact that it expressed views which Latin Americans wanted to hear," views arising from their fear of North American power. The negative effect of the book, "repeated *ad nauseum*," was to create a myth of an uncultured, materialistic United States. On a positive note, *Ariel* encouraged educational reform, and a "Latin-American ideal gave intellectuals a higher sense of purpose than narrow nationalism could ever have done." Basic Rodó library.

Goldberg, Isaac. "José Enrique Rodó (1872–1917)." In *Studies in Spanish American Literature*. With an introduction by J. D. M. Ford. New York: Brentano's Publishers, 1920.

An ardent admirer of Rodó, and of *Ariel*, Goldberg sums up: "The Rodó of *Ariel* . . . is a perspicacious, patient thinker, moderate in judgment, moderate in counsel, tolerant in attitude, glowing with a constant, rather than a volcanic, passion for justice and freedom. His style is eminently matched to his subject."

González Echevarría, Roberto. "The Case of the Speaking Statue:

Ariel and the Magisterial Rhetoric of the Latin American Essay." In *The Voice of the Masters: Writing and Authority in Modern Latin American Literature*. Austin: University of Texas Press, 1985.

González Echevarría asks, "How can we account for the presence of *Ariel* in today's Latin American literature?" and answers that its relevancy is "due not only to the resiliency of the figures explicitly set on stage, but also to the way in which these figures engage in a polemical interplay beneath the surface of the essay." He adds a new dimension by revealing that "*Ariel*'s generic identification lies with the classical dialogue," and with similar insight details the symbolism of the qualities associated with Ariel: "air, spirit, and voice." González Echevarría also explores the hidden but implicit violence in Rodó's message to the youth of Latin America and ends with the significance of a baroque interpretation of Rodó's metaphor of the hospitable king. This examination of "magisterial rhetoric" is the most important contemporary essay on the subject of *Ariel*. Essential for Rodó library.

Lewis, Bart L. "Sarmiento, Martí, and Rodó: Three Views of the United States in the Latin American Essay." In *Portrayal of America in Various Literatures*. Edited by Walodymyr T. Zyla and Robert G. Collmer. Lubbock: Texas Tech University Press, 1978.

Lewis describes *Ariel* as considered and earnest, "the opinion of a man who soberly examines cultural differences and concludes that material progress in North America has been gained at the expense of the sublime, and Latin America is well advised not to do likewise."

Silvert, Kalman H. "*Ariel* and the Dilemma of the Intellectuals." In *The Conflict Society*. Rev. ed. New York: American Universities Field Staff, 1966.

A subchapter to "Part Three. Intellectuals and Their Inquietudes." Silvert quotes extensively from the last third of *Ariel*, in his own translation, and says, "The book, still widely viewed in Latin America as an accurate portrayal of American democracy, is also a required part of any discussion of Latin American political thought." At the same time, he believes that "time has passed by" much of Rodó's political commentary. The main focus of the chapter is Uruguay. Basic Rodó library.

Stabb, Martin S. *In Quest of Identity: Patterns in the Spanish-American Essay of Ideas, 1890–1960.* Chapel Hill: University of North Carolina Press, 1967.

Stabb's basic study does not devote a separate chapter to Rodó, but Rodó and *Arielismo* are prominent, especially in the chapter "The Revolt against Scientism."

Torres-Ríoseco, Arturo. "José Enrique Rodó." In *New World Literature: Tradition and Revolt in Latin America.* Berkeley & Los Angeles: University of California Press, 1949.

Torres Ríoseco identifies Rodó as the product of French critical theory, marking in prose, "as positively as Rubén Darío in poetry, the constant orientation toward the French spirit. . . . We cannot but esteem this generous contribution to esthetic evaluation, this new manifestation of poetic style applied to a discipline of rigid concepts and cold formulae." He deems *Ariel* "Rodó's masterpiece."

———. "José Enrique Rodó and His Idealistic Philosophy." In *Aspects of Spanish-American Literature.* Seattle: University of Washington Press, 1963.

Torres-Ríoseco, at this later date, considers Rodó's masterpiece to be *Motivos de Proteo,* but lists *Ariel* as "his greatest contribution to Latin-American culture." Chapter is largely a synthesis of *Ariel* (English quotations from Stimson translation). Torres-Ríoseco regrets that "Latin America has not fulfilled the hopes created by Rodó's vision. . . ," and that "it would be a mockery to speak of aesthetic ideals, of *otium,* among illiterate and oppressed peoples." With Rodó, Torres-Ríoseco believes that "North America will transform its materialistic impulses into purer forms of existence . . . and that out of its own ruined societies, Latin America will build the noble architecture of the New World."

Essays in Journals

Antuña, José G. "Rodó's *Ariel.*" *Americas* 13 (1961).

Somewhat diffuse generalist article. Appraises state of Latin American culture in 1961. Focuses on questions of "Americanness" and American relations with Europe. Nothing in depth regarding *Ariel.*

Arencibia-Huidobro, Yolanda. "The Modern Concept of Latin America." *Cultures* 5 (1978).

A tentative bibliography of readings intended to define and illuminate Latin America. Excerpts from Rodó. Compiled and with a preface by Arturo Ardao. Havana: Casa de las Américas, 1977.

Bacheller, Cecil C. "An Introduction for Studies on Rodó." *Hispania* 46 (1963).

Brief résumé of the Rodó canon. Reviews various critical commentaries. Suggests that "four decades" after Rodó's death, critics may take a more "impersonal" view of this writer, aided by increasing organization of his papers in the Archivo de Rodó. Little relevance to *Ariel*.

———. "Rodó's Ideas on the Relationship of Beauty and Morality." *Canadian Modern Language Review* 19 (1962–1963).

Discusses Rodó's aesthetic, based on *Ariel* and other writings: "He would agree with Plato that beauty disposes men toward right conduct and right thinking. . . . With Kant he would say that the appreciation of beauty is a symptom of a highly developed morality." No critical stance.

———. "Rodó's Philosophy of the Personality." *Xavier University Studies* 2 (1963).

Argument based exclusively on *Motivos de Proteo*.

Barcos, Julio R. "Our Professors of Idealism in America. Notes for a Critical Essay upon the Positive and Negative Values of Our Indo-Spanish Culture." *Inter América* 3, 2 (1915).

Barcos calls Rodó the "Apostle of Greco-Latinism" and attributes to him "the wisest aphorism of the period: *to reform is to live*." At the same time, however, Barcos affirms that Rodó was "sowing the false idealism of barren results." He recounts the deplorable social conditions that have produced not a superbut a subrace and counters Rodó's philosophical proposal with the statement, "We are the Philistines, and the true idealists are the Americans of the North." Very early opposition to hypothesis of *Ariel*.

Earle, Peter G. "Utopia, Universopolis, Macondo." *Hispanic Review* 50 (1982).

Brief mention of Rodó's *Ariel* and *Motivos de Proteo* as examples of the long association of Latin America with the myth of Utopia. Notwithstanding the hopeful visions of Rodó and others, however, "the Latin American mind has seldom been seriously drawn to Utopia. Deliverance is sought in the magical view [of García Márquez and Carlos Fuentes, among others]." Contemporary Latin American literature, Earle argues in this excellent essay, "spurns the reason of state and the state-making dream."

Gracia, Jorge J. E., and Ivan A. Jaksic. "The Problem of Philosophical Identity in Latin America." *Revista Interamericana de Bibliografía* 34, 1 (1984).

The authors examine the often-debated question: "Is there, or can there be, a Latin American philosophy?" Their answer, "as any good philosophical answer," is both affirmative and negative. In a review of the history of Latin American thought, Rodó is cited as an early opponent of Positivist optimism in regard to industrialization, who used the Ariel-Caliban symbolism as "an instrument for social analysis."

Hayes, Francis. "Essays, Upheavals and Mr. Nixon." *South Atlantic Bulletin* 14, 4 (1959).

In a brief, but very pointed, commentary, Francis Hayes suggests an overlooked explanation for the upheavals resulting from Vice-President Richard Nixon's visit to "Indo-Hispanic America": "an essay entitled *Ariel*." Hayes classifies Rodó as one of the writers most responsible for the "distorted image of Uncle Sam" now held by Latin Americans. He proposes that *Ariel* might appropriately take its place on our bookshelves alongside *Common Sense, Das Kapital*, and other "upheaval-inducing literature."

Krenn, Michael L. "'Lions in the Woods': The United States Confronts Economic Nationalism in Latin America, 1917–1929." *Radical History Review* 33 (1985).

Brief mention of *Ariel* as an example of Latin American resentment of the "Colossus of the North." The article is an analysis of U.S.–Latin American relations during the postwar years in terms of the North American economic presence and the concurrent development of economic nationalism.

Langhorst, Rick. "Caliban in America." *Journal of Spanish Studies: Twentieth Century* 8, 1–2 (1980).

Langhorst traces the borrowing of Shakespeare's Caliban

through Latin American literature, citing Rodó's use as "the best known Latin American adoption of Caliban," adding that from the outset, "Rodó's attempt to transfer Shakespearian symbolism breaks down." In spite of that perceived deficiency, he concedes that "the repercussions of this slim volume were both immediate and long-lasting."

Langhorst poses as the antithesis of *Ariel* Roberto Fernández Retamar's *Calibán*. In a "reverse homage to Rodó, Caliban now represents the oppressed."

Maetzú, Ramiro de. "Rodó and the United States." *Inter-America* 9, 5 (1926).

A Spaniard's view of the United States. Maetzú reports that "the ideas that prevail among cultured men in Latin countries concerning the United States are still more or less identical with those expressed . . . in *Ariel*." Then he outlines conditions that have changed and prophecies that were erroneous—principally, that, contrary to Rodó's scornful opinion, "the axis of the world" has been diverted toward a new capital: "Today the world revolves between New York and San Francisco."

Núñez Harrell, Elizabeth. "Caliban: A Positive Symbol for Third-World Writers." *Obsidian* 8 (1982).

Núñez Harrell's thesis is that for many Caribbean and Latin American writers, "identification with Calibán is vital . . . because he is a positive image of the first natives of the New World to be colonized by the European." Relevant to Ariel only in that this represents a change in attitude from Latin American identification with Ariel following the publication of Rodó's essay.

Reid, John T. "The Rise and Decline of the Ariel-Caliban Antithesis in Spanish America." *The Americas* 34, 3 (1978).

Excellent survey and analysis of the "international political resonance" of the Ariel-Caliban contraposition, cataloguing changing viewpoints. Reid argues that although the metaphor still has "currency in some *anti-yanqui* circles, it has not lasted well with many thoughtful intellectuals." He concludes, however, "I do not want to leave the impression that his symbolism . . . has entirely lost its potency in Spanish America"; and, here Reid quotes Kalman Silvert, "Rodó still touches chords of sympathy and desire in Latin America."

Salomon, Noel. "Cosmopolitanism and Internationalism in the History of Ideas in Latin America." *Cultures* 6 (1979).

Salomon's subtitle is "Toward a Definition of Cosmopolitanism." He finds the first negative use of the term in chapter 5 of *Ariel*. Rodó, he believes, saw cosmopolitanism as "an impoverishing mingling with uncultivated foreigners . . . destroying what was genuinely . . . Uruguayan." Salomon attributes subsequent opposition between "cosmopolitanism" and "Latin-American" to this source.

Symington, James W. "Echoes of Rodó." In *Americas* 20, 3 (March 1968).

This early North American recognition of Rodó by then Chief of Protocol Symington studies the relationship between black unrest in the 1960s and political instability in Latin America. A thoughtful examination of Rodó's ideas.

Van Aken, Mark J. "The Radicalization of the Uruguayan Student Movement." *The Americas* 33, 1 (1976).

Excellent essay describing the central roles played by the Ariel Student Center (named in honor of Rodó, whose death in 1917 coincided with a student strike) and the magazine *Ariel*. Van Aken describes the strange tensions between Rodoist idealism portrayed in the pages of *Ariel* and growing interest in the leftist and proletarian leaders of Europe and America, as well as the steadily leftist progression of the politics of the Ariel Center.

———. "Rodó, *Ariel*, and Student Militants of Uruguay." In *Homage to Irving Leonard: Essays on Hispanic Art, History and Literature*. Edited by Raquel Chang-Rodríguez and Donald B. Yates. East Lansing: Latin American Studies Center, Michigan State University, 1977.

Closely related to the previous article, this essay is more narrowly focused. Van Aken reports that for militant Uruguayan students in the late twenties, Rodó's conservative values were rapidly becoming obsolete. This student view was perhaps best expressed by Héctor González Areosa, quoted here: "'Elegant stylizations' had been satisfying to Rodó but were no longer adequate for a younger generation facing 'concrete problems of sociology, politics, and culture.'"

Whitaker, Arthur P. "*Ariel* on Caliban in Both Americas." In

Homage to Irving Leonard: Essays on Hispanic Art, History and Literature. Edited by Raquel Chang-Rodríguez and Donald B. Yates. East Lansing: Latin American Studies Center, Michigan State University, 1977.

Whitaker takes exception to the interpretations of two earlier analysts of *Ariel,* Hubert Herring and David Green, and argues that Rodó "aimed his fire at Calibanism not only in the U.S. . . . but also among Latin Americans. . . , and that *Ariel* came under increasingly heavy counterfire from Rodó's fellow Latin Americans" and was *not* "sacred writ" (quoting Green) for generations. Therefore, when in 1974 Secretary of State Henry Kissinger closed his address to the OAS with a quotation from *Ariel,* the time was already past when he might "hope to gain favor by invoking the authority of Rodó."

Zum Felde, Alberto. "José Enrique Rodó: His Place among the Thinkers of America." *Inter-America* 7, 4 (1924).

This article was published in Spanish in 1921, in *Crítica de la literatura uruguaya.* Zum Felde, subjecting the man and his writings to a drastic criticism, attacks prevalent opinion that Rodó is a stylist and leading man of letters. A seminal essay in Rodó studies.

Translations

"Ariel." [A fragment] translated by Willis Knapp Jones. *Spanish American Literature in Translation.* Edited by W. K. Jones. New York: Frederick Ungar, 1963.

"A Dialogue between Bronze and Marble." José Enrique Rodó. *Inter-America* 1, 4 (1917).

History and ideas of art in the guise of a dialogue between two classic sculptures, Michelangelo's *David* and Benvenuto Cellini's *Perseus.*

The Motives of Proteus. Introduction by Havelock Ellis. Translated by Angel Flores. London: Allen & Unwin, 1929. [New York: Gordon Press, 1977].

"Rodó: An Evocation of the Spirit of *Ariel.*" Armando Donoso. *Inter-America* 1, 1 (1917).

Fragments of *Ariel* interwoven in an imaginary "dialogue with the Master."

In Spanish and Portuguese

*Works containing a significant bibliography.

Books

*Albarrán Puente, Glicerio. *El pensamiento de José Enrique Rodó.* Madrid: Ediciones Cultura Hispánica, 1953.

Albarrán Puente is interested in Rodó's intellectual formation, set against the general background of Hispanic philosophical currents. Good chronology and bibliography. Basic Rodó library.

Andrade Coello, Alejandro. *Rodó.* Quito: Imprenta y Encuadernaciones Nacionales, 1917.

Personal reminiscences and meditations occasioned by receipt of a cable stating, "Rodó has died in Rome." Comments on *Ariel* are largely paraphrases of text.

Antuña, José Gervacio. *Un panorama del espíritu: En el cincuentenario de "Ariel".* Montevideo: Editorial Florensa y Lafón, 1952.

It is Antuña's intent "to summarize, in brief sections" encompassing all the world events of the years 1900 to 1950, "the trajectory of *Ariel* through the [Latin] American spirit." A large and ambitious book undercut by the subjective and fragmentary nature of the argument.

Ardao, Arturo. *Estudios latinoamericanos: Historia de las ideas.* Caracas: Monte Avila, 1978.

The author lists the so-called charges against Rodó (such as hostility toward science and its technical applications), then responds to these charges in an attempt to "clarify the record." Brief outline of the six parts of *Ariel*. Considers that Prospero's discourse is an effort to determine the autonomy of Latin America and to define its culture.

———. *Orígenes de la influencia de Renan en el Uruguay.* Montevideo: Ministerio de Instrucción Pública, 1955.

Placing the apogee of Renan's influence in Rodó's *Ariel*, Ardao suggests a history of influence, beginning with mention in 1862 in an article published by Adolfo Vaillant. He demonstrates particularly the effect of Renan's *La vida de Jesús*, translated in 1863.

———. *Rodó, su americanismo.* Montevideo: Biblioteca de Marcha, 1970.

Ardao examines Rodó's Americanism in literary, cultural, political, and heroic contexts. *Ariel*, in his view, is of primary importance as cultural influence.

Arias, Alejandro. *Ideario de Rodó*. Salto: La Junta Directiva del Ateneo, 1938.

A series of lectures. For Arias, *Arielismo* is a moral philosophy too pure to be heard by the "Calibanesque ears of the anonymous masses." At the same time, in a period in which Spain is "bleeding," the message of *Ariel* is still to be heeded, in order that culture "not founder in a sea of meaningless words."

Barbagelata, Hugo D. *Una centuria literaria, 1800–1900*. Paris: Biblioteca Latino Americana, n.d. (prologue signed 1923).

Barbagelata says of Rodó: "He was not a master from Uruguay, nor a master from the region of the River Plate; he was the master of all those who speak Spanish." The collection contains fragments from Rodó's most important works, including *Ariel*.

*Benedetti, Mario. *Genio y figura de José Enrique Rodó*. Buenos Aires: Editorial Universitaria de Buenos Aires, 1966.

Excellent resource following the usual format of the *Genio y figura* series: chronology, life, works, place in literary history, bibliography. In assessing the importance of Rodó, Benedetti quotes Pedro Henríquez Ureña's judgment that Rodó "was perhaps the first to influence us through the written word alone." Good discussion of various polemics concerning *Ariel*, including Rodó's "myopia" in regard to the Indian and his blindness with respect to imperialism. Basic Rodó library.

Bollo, Sarah. *Sobre José Enrique Rodó*. Montevideo: Imp. Uruguaya, 1946.

Two separate but related studies: "Ariel and the Latin World," and "An Evaluation of Rodó." In the former, Bollo argues that criticisms made of *Arielismo* from 1900 to 1950 are unfounded; *Ariel* illustrates the continuation of Latinness as adapted to American realities. As an evaluation: more than philosopher, Rodó was the artist supreme.

Botelho Gosálvez, Raúl. *Reflexiones sobre el cincuentenario del 'Ariel' de José Enrique Rodó*. La Paz: n.p., 1960.

Slight (actually a lecture) re-evaluation of the hemispheric political background against which Rodó presented his *Ariel:* "a somber picture." The author's thesis is that the United States no longer is represented by Caliban; that the "Good Neighbor Policy" has led to pan-Americanism. (Ironically, one of the negative aspects of the turn-of-the-century Caliban, according to Botelho Gosálvez, was U.S. intervention in Nicaragua.)

Callorda, Pedro Erasmo. *Films: Evocando el pasado*. Lima: n.p., 1939.

Personal reminiscences recalling Rodó's inarguable power in approving or disapproving books that came to his attention; Rodó's participation in the national House of Deputies; Callorda's delight in meeting Rodó, as well as Rodó's lukewarm approbation of his work; and Callorda's experiences in Mexico at the time of Rodó's death.

Camelo Torres, Salvador. *José Enrique Rodó*. Mexico City: Cuadernos de Lectura Popular, 1967.

Very small book with brief mention of *Ariel*: "It succeeded in 'shaking up' public opinion," and was the "source of new ideas." "It exists. It lives." Excerpts from writings that succeeded *Ariel*.

Costabile de Amorín, Helena, and Mariá del Rosario Fernández Alonso. *Rodó: Pensador y estilista*. Montevideo: Academia Nacional de Letras, 1973.

A rereading of Rodó's writings on the centenary of his birth, undertaken "in the light of the circumstances of the world in which we live, in order to be more than ever sensitive to the need . . . to return to our origins, from which emerges Iberoamerican culture in particular, and American in general." *Ariel*, in the authors' view, set the great themes of Rodó's historical-political meditations.

Escardo, Florencio. *Ariel o el discípulo*. Buenos Aires: Instituto Amigos del Libro Argentino, 1962.

Half this study, focused on broad aesthetics, is dedicated to Pinocchio and Peter Pan. The sense of the study is to consider the total implications of the figures of Ariel and Caliban in Latin American literature, not merely their application in Rodó's *Ariel*.

Gallinal, Gustavo. *Crítica y arte*. Montevideo: Editorial Uruguaya, 1920.

An examination of Rodó's "beautiful prose style," which necessarily results from "clarity of logic, passion for ideas, intelligence and creative imagination, vast culture, and conviction." Gallinal discusses the influence of Renan and Bourget and Rodó's rejection of those writers who might "cloud his faith" in the endurance of the norms that defined (Latin) American society.

———. *Rodó*. Montevideo: Renacimiento, 1918.

A lecture delivered by Gallinal on December 3, 1917, reviewing the broad literary scene and focusing to a large degree on the work of Rodó. Perhaps most interesting as the catalyst for the response of Raúl Montero Bustamente. (See Montero Bustamente, *José Enrique Rodó: Carta al Dr. Gustavo Gallinal*)

García Godoy, F. *Americanismo literario: José Martí, José Enrique Rodó, F. García Calderón, R. Blanco-Fombona*. Madrid: Editorial América, n.d.

García Godoy's thesis is that the "intellectual infancy" of Latin America was of long duration and that during that time Latins were easily seduced by the song of foreign sirens. In the figures of his study, he sees an emerging "literary Americanism." The section on Rodó is the most substantial of the four. He calls *Ariel* the "spiritual breviary of Spanish American youth."

Giraldi, Nora. *Rodó. Con comentario completo de Ariel*. Montevideo [?]: Editorial Técnica, n.d.

From a series, "Manuales de literatura," this slim book outlines basic information about the literary world of Rodó's Uruguay, his life and work. The principal content is a very elementary explication of *Ariel*.

[Homenaje] *Cervantes* (May, 1918).

On the first anniversary of his death, a collection of "opinions" on Rodó, with a conscious emphasis on universality—each author signs both name and country. Of greatest literary interest is the opening piece, by Rubén Darío, whose name is often linked with that of Rodó. Also of passing interest, "Rodó's Last Interview," with the Argentine Julián de Charras, and Rodó's impressions of Barcelona, where he stopped on his way to Italy, the place of his death.

Homenaje a José Enrique Rodó. Edited by Maximino García. Revista *Ariel*, Organo del centro de Estudiantes "Ariel." Montevideo, 1920.

Interesting collection of tributes delivered at the ceremonies accompanying Rodó's burial, and on various anniversaries of his death. Basic Rodó library.

Homenaje a José Enrique Rodó. Breve reseña de su vida y su obra. Edited by Carlos Sabat Ercasty. Montevideo: Imprenta la Rápida, 1942.

Small volume containing a "Hymn to Rodó" written by the editor, biographical and critical notes, and fragmentary excerpts from Rodó's works.

[Homenaje]. *Nosotros* 11, 26 (1917). A special issue dedicated, by the editors Alfredo A. Bianchi and Roberto F. Giusti, to Rodó on his death. The editors state that the issue "is not intended to be a blind glorification but, rather, a careful weighing of the work left by the Master." The majority of pieces, however, as may be expected, are eulogistic.

* *José Enrique Rodó: Actuación parlamentaria.* Edited by Dr. Jorge A. Silva Cencio. Montevideo: n.p., 1972.

This enormous compilation of Rodó's activities in the Uruguayan Chamber of Deputies (Cámara de Senadores) was published by the Chamber on the occasion of the centenary of Rodó's birth. In light of *Ariel,* it is interesting that Rodó mentions the United States very seldom during three legislative terms.

* Julio, Jaime Julia. *Rodó y Santo Domingo (Recopilación).* Santo Domingo: n.p., 1971.

This collection of letters to and from Rodó, and eclectic reprinted articles, is intended as a testimonial to the national admiration of Rodó. Not arranged as bibliography, it is nonetheless a good bibliographical source for scattered articles.

Júlio, Sílvio. *José Enrique Rodó e o cinqüentenário do seu libro "Ariel."* Rio de Janeiro: Ministério da Educação e Cultura, 1954.

Focusing on the "intellectual ambiance" and "nucleus and form" of *Ariel,* Julio invokes God's miracle: to "introduce into Brazil . . . the most noble ideals that José Enrique Rodó defended in the pages of his immaculate book."

Jurado Toro, Bernardo. *José Enrique Rodó: "El hispanoamericano."* Caracas: Ediciones del Banco del Caribe, 1974.

Life, work, influences, a traditional format, in addition to

Rodó's "concept of Americanism" and his "style and originality." Jurado considers *Ariel* the book that will always be associated with the name of Rodó.

Lago, Julio. *El verdadero Rodó: Estudios críticos*. Montevideo, 1973.
Twenty-eight brief essays on various aspects of Rodó's writings, including a fictionalized dialogue based on *Ariel*, incorporating characters as diverse as the Inca Garcilaso and John Adams. Basic thesis: that literary modes are cyclical, and that Rodó is again emerging as a writer whose work will endure.

Lasplaces, Alberto. *Opiniones literarias (Prosistas uruguayos contemporáneos)*. Prologue by Víctor Pérez Petit. Montevideo: Claudio García, 1919.
Among writers considered are Horacio Quiroga, Carlos Reyles, Florencio Sánchez, and Javier de Viana. In Lasplaces' opinion, Rodó was the victim of self-suggestion, and the error that converts *Ariel* "into a simple literary sermon lacking major transcendental consequences for life" was having given too much importance to the symbol of Ariel without conceding the reality of Caliban. He defends a "noisily youthful United States," whose "mind is cleared of the cobwebs of tradition." An early negation of the "seduction" of Rodó's prose.

Lauxar (Osvaldo Crispo Acosta). *Rubén Darío y José Enrique Rodó*. Montevideo: Agencia General de Librería y Publicaciones, 1924. A revised version of *Motivos de crítica hispanoamericana*. Montevideo: Imprenta Mercurio, 1914.
Not, as suggested by the title, a comparative study, but long biographical/critical essays on each writer. In reference to *Ariel*, the author emphasizes Rodó's dependence on Renan and concludes that there is little to suggest that the republican government Rodó dreamed of would ever be a reality. Of Rodó's style, Lauxar suggests that architecture is a more meaningful analogue than music.

Lockhart, Washington. *Rodó: Vigencia de su pensamiento en América*. Mercedes: Uruguay, 1964.
Eighteen-page essay awarded Uruguayan Press Prize for best essay of 1963 published on "Living Presence of Rodó in America." Argument: that "soul of Rodó" can aid in restoring Hispanism.

————. *Rodó y su prédica: Sentimientos fundamentales*. Montevideo: Ediciones de la Banda Oriental, 1982.

Lockhart argues that all Rodó's writing can be reduced to a single intent: his "unflagging effort" to communicate "his vision of the world and of the life he experienced with rare intensity." He urges that *Ariel* be read in the context of all Rodó's work and emphasizes the "aristocracy of the worker" and the role of action in that treatise.

Martínez Durán, Carlos. *José Enrique Rodó. En el espíritu de su tiempo y en la conciencia de América*. Caracas: Imprenta Universitaria, 1974.

An homage on the centenary of Rodó's birth (1871–1971). The author urges a careful consideration of Rodó's work, the "validity of its message," even in the midst of "attacks and undervaluation" in the year of the centenary. He quotes Arturo Ardao—"Rodó has suffered everything, except oblivion"—and places himself squarely in the camp of admirers.

Montero Bustamente, Raúl. *José Enrique Rodó: Carta al Dr. Gustavo Gallinal*. Montevideo: La Buena Prensa, 1918.

A tiny (nineteen-page) oddity: a publication in form of a letter addressed to Gustavo Gallinal, which must be one of the first negative reactions to Rodó's eminence. The letter criticizes Rodó's "imprecision," his failure to perceive the "essential solution," even his lack of appreciation for women: "because he was able to admire woman only through the sovereign and chaste nakedness of the Venus de Milo." Obviously a lonely voice in the general clamorous acclaim for Rodó.

Oribe, Emilio, ed. *Rodó, estudio crítico y antología*. Buenos Aires: Editorial Losada, 1971.

Brief excerpts from a number of Rodó's works. Oribe's critical judgment is that Rodó "enjoys an uneclipsed living presence," and that, along with Sarmiento and Montalvo, he forms "the highest flowering of prose and thought in our America."

Penco, Wilfredo. *José Enrique Rodó*. Montevideo [?]: Arca Editorial, 1978.

Brief life and works, including interesting photographs and mementos reproduced for the first time. Chronology of life.

* Pereda, Clemente. *Magna patria. Rodó: Su vida y su obra*. Caracas: n.p., 1973.

This large but piecemeal study encompasses most of Rodó's writings and much of his philosophy and aesthetic. The author's opinions are difficult to isolate, but clearly laudatory.

Pérez Petit, Víctor. *Rodó; Su vida. Su obra*. Montevideo: Imprenta Latina, 1918.

An early biographical "portrait" by a contemporary and friend. Subjective, but for students of Rodó, his era, the literature of the period, Pérez Petit's many personal anecdotes are a rich source. Basic Rodó library.

Reyes de Viana, Celia, and Celia I. Viana Reyes. *José Enrique Rodó: "Genio" educador iberoamericano*. Montevideo: División General de Extensión Universitaria, 1980.

A disconnected attempt to extract from Rodó's various themes and works the unifying element of Rodó-the-educator.

Rodó y sus críticos. Edited by Hugo D. Barbagelata. Paris: Imprenta Vertongen, 1920.

A laudatory preface by the editor precedes a group of personal and critical articles by Spanish, French, and Latin American writers, including Rubén Darío, Miguel de Unamuno, and Alfonso Reyes. Of interest as much for the commentators as for the content.

Salva, Juana María. *Rodó para los escolares. Epítome de su vida y breve glosa de sus ideas*. Montevideo: Editorial Ombú, 1941. A handbook for schoolchildren, extolling a national hero. It is, in fact, reading "recommended by the National Council for Primary and Secondary Education."

Sánchez, Luis Amador. *Cuatro estudios: Hostos, Martí, Rodó, Blanco-Fombona*. São Paulo: Universidade de São Paulo, 1958. (Separata of *Língua e literatura espanhola e hispano-americana*, Boletim 140.)

Sánchez quotes Miguel Uzcátegui Balza, who during the Second World War had called Rodó the "intellectual past, present, and future of America," an opinion with which he concurs. "Rodó signifies strength and hope; he is a lifebuoy for our age of exhaustion."

*Silva Cencio, Jorge A. *Rodó y la legislación social*. Montevideo: Biblioteca de Marcha, 1973.

Unlike Silva Cencio's 1972 compilation of all the texts and references of Rodó's activities as a legislator, this volume is an *analysis* of Rodó's contributions to the development of social legislation in Uruguay, as both a literary and a political figure. Extensive notes and interesting bibliographical references divided by category (Rodó as critic, aspects of his personality, and others) and by reference to individual works.

Seré de Berro, María. *José Enrique Rodó: Su mensaje*. Montevideo: n.p., 1974.

Very elementary reading of the life and work of the "Maestro de la Juventud." Intended for use as a text, to clarify the "complex concepts" in Rodó's works, "especially *Ariel*."

Torrano, Hugo. *Rodó: acción y libertad. Restauración de su imagen*. Montevideo: Barreiro y Ramos, 1973.

Recognizing that Rodó has been "unjustly criticized for political-ideological motives," Torrano's intent is, through "unprejudiced discussion," to explain Rodó to contemporary readers. Extensive notes.

Zaldumbide, Gonzalo. *Cuatro clásicos americanos: Rodó, Montalvo, Fray Gaspar de Villarroel, P. J. B. Aguirre*. Madrid: Ediciones Cultura Hispánica, 1957.

A peculiar assemblage. The author's introduction is confined to remarks on Rodó, an assessment of what is lasting in Rodó's writings. His judgment is that Rodó will survive the "profusion of praise" that eclipsed his tomb, owing to his mastery of art and his fusion of realism and idealism.

———. *José Enrique Rodó*. New York/Paris: Revue Hispanique, 1921. A slightly defensive view of Latin American culture and literature written by a contemporary. Places Rodó in context; discusses his intellectual formation and, superficially, the body of his writing. Zaldumbide considers *Ariel* the source of "modern idealism" in Latin America. Romantic and subjective musing on Rodó, the man, and his world.

———. *José Enrique Rodó*. Montevideo: Biblioteca de la Academia Nacional de Letras, 1967.

A reprint of the earlier study, published on the occasion of an homage to Zaldumbide offered by the Uruguayan Academy. The first third of the volume is a panegyric dedicated to the "prominent Ecuadorian critic of Rodó."

————. *José Enrique Rodó; su personalidad y su obra*. Madrid: Editorial América, 1919.

According to a prefatory note in the 1921 edition, a pirated version of *José Enrique Rodó*. Identical text.

————. *Montalvo y Rodó*. New York: Instituto de las Españas, 1938.

See *Cuatro clásicos*. With the exception of the first two paragraphs, the text is identical, although the chapters and chapter headings are differently arranged. The Montalvo piece is also the same.

Essays in Books

Ardao, Arturo. "La conciencia filosófica de Rodó." In *La literatura uruguaya del 900. Número 2* (1950).

A special edition of the journal *Número*. The "Generation of 900" included, in addition to Rodó, Carlos Vaz Ferreira, Julio Herrera y Reissig, Florencio Sánchez, Delmira Agustini, Javier de Viana, and Horacio Quiroga.

————. "José Enrique Rodó." In *La filosofía en el Uruguay en el siglo XX*. Mexico City: Fondo de Cultura Económica, 1956.

Included in section entitled "Philosophy of Experience."

Carbonell, Miguel Angel. "José Enrique Rodó." In *Hombres de nuestra América*. Prologue by Ismael Clark. Havana: Imprenta "La Prueba," 1915.

Carbonell describes Rodó as "living on the peak of the literary mountain like some unsullied god." He praises Rodó not for being one who "uses polished and sonorous phrases empty of meaning" but, rather, for casting his ideas in the "mold of rational philosophy."

Esquenazi-Mayo, Roberto. "Revaloración de Rodó." In *Actas del Primer Congreso Internacional de Hispanistas*. Oxford: Dolphin Book Co., 1964.

An argument questioning some of Rodó's criticisms of the United States. The author's thesis is that Rodó was a "modernist writer," not "a prophet." Rodó erred (to some degree, perhaps, because unlike Sarmiento and Martí he had never visited the United States) in his denigration of North American cultural, moral, and artistic accomplishments.

Filartigas, Juan M. "José Enrique Rodó." In *Artistas del Uruguay. Impresiones literarias.*

First chapter in small book also containing essays on Herrera y Reissig, Delmira Agustini, Emilio Frugoni, and Juana de Ibarbourou. In *Ariel* "Rodó . . . effects a perfect manual for spiritual education which should be in the hands of every youth."

Frugoni, Emilio. "La orientación espiritual de Rodó." In *La sensibilidad americana.* Montevideo: Editor Maximino García, n.d.

Four brief articles published at the time of the return of Rodó's remains to Uruguay; an impassioned defense against charges that Rodó was a reactionary.

García Calderón, Francisco. "Ariel y Caliban." In *Hombres e ideas de nuestro tiempo.* Valencia: F. Sempere, n.d. (prologue by Emile Boutroux is dated 1907).

A collection of essays published in Lima between 1904 and 1907, plus four previously unpublished pieces, all related to "social problems." García Calderón traces the figures of Ariel and Caliban through Shakespeare and Renan to Rodó, whose treatise, to him, recalls William James and deLavisse.

García Calderón, Ventura. "Rodó. Significación de 'Ariel.'" In *Indice crítico de la literatura hispanoamericana. Los ensayistas.* Mexico City: Editorial Guaranía, 1954.

Chapter 5, Book 3, under the general heading, "The Reign of Scientific Positivism."

———. *Semblanzas de América.* Madrid: Biblioteca Ariel, 1920.

Rodó is the subject of the first essay, followed by eleven individual studies and a note on Uruguayan romanticism.

González, Ariosto D. "Rodó, su bibliografía y sus críticos." In *Política y letras.* Montevideo: José M. Serrano, 1937.

Following a brief introductory reminiscence, the essay is essentially a commentary on the major Rodó bibliography compiled by Arturo Scarone. González summarizes a number of critical appraisals of Rodó's writings. (Also the prologue to the Scarone edition.)

González-Blanco, Andrés. "José Enrique Rodó: Crítico." In *Escritores representativos de América.* Madrid: Editorial América,

n.d. (prologue is signed 1917).
Five individual studies, of which "José Enrique Rodó" is the first.

Henríquez Ureña, Pedro. "Ariel." In *Obra crítica*. Mexico City: Fondo de Cultura Económica, 1960.
Emphasizing that he is not the first, Henríquez Ureña calls Rodó "the most brilliant stylist in the Spanish tongue." He classifies *Ariel* as a sociophilosophical essay and predicts that it will keep "the eyes of a generation fixed on a great ideal." (This essay also appears in *Selección de ensayos* [Havana: Casa de las Américas, 1965].)

Maggi, Carlos. "Calibán 63." In *El Uruguay y su gente*. Montevideo: Editorial Alfa, 1967.
A collection of essays addressing the problems, and their possible solutions, of contemporary life in Uruguay. Maggi laments the tendency "to nurture and keep under glass" the "enchanting but absolutely worthless orchid" symbolizing the world of Rodó, now disappeared. He ends with the often-quoted words: "Gentlemen: Close the tomb of *Ariel* with seven padlocks . . . and forward."

Real de Azúa, Carlos. *Historia visible e historia esotérica: Personajes y claves del debate latinoamericano*. Montevideo: Arca Editorial, 1975.
A collection of essays by various essayists, among them, Martínez Estrada, Sarmiento, Vasconcelos, and Luis Alberto Sánchez, on the subject of the "ills" of Latin America. Three essays are devoted to Rodó, an excellent review and commentary on the series of "rereadings" of *Ariel* since its publication in 1900. Real de Azúa sees Rodó's dual identity as artist and thinker as one of the major problems in evaluating his work.

Sánchez, Luis Alberto. *Balance y liquidación de novecientos*. Santiago: Ediciones Ercilla, 1941.
The chapter devoted to Rodó begins: "Spoiled child of an old and wealthy family . . ." The essay emphasizes Rodó's privileged situation and how that position relates to his views of the exquisite. The overall sense of the study is that any negativity in regard to Rodó's generation will serve to foment an affirmative and healthy reaction.

Vitier, Medardo. "El mensaje de Rodó." In *Del ensayo americano*. Mexico City: Fondo de Cultura Económica, 1945.
Based on three themes: culture; racial, political, and economic problems; and a sense of nationalism.

Zubillaga, Juan Antonio. "Ariel." In *Crítica literaria*. Montevideo: A. Monteverde & Cía, 1914.
The author devotes nine chapters in this collection to Rodó. Of *Ariel* Zubillaga states, "The elevation of the thought corresponds to the magnificence of the style," and adds that it contains the germ of many of Rodó's central ideas.

Zum Felde, Alberto. "José Enrique Rodó." In *Crítica de la literatura uruguaya*. Montevideo: Imp. El Siglo Ilustrado, n.d. (preliminary note dated 1921).

———. "José Enrique Rodó." In *Proceso intelectual de Uruguay, y crítica de su literatura*. Montevideo: Editorial Claridad, 1941.

Essays in Journals

This listing does not attempt to include the hundreds of articles on Rodó and *Ariel*, merely to record some items not widely identified, or those appearing following publication of major bibliographies.

Aguilera-Malta, Demetrio. "Actualidad de *Ariel*." *Comunidad Latinoamericana de Escritores Boletín* 12 (1972).

Altamirano, Carlos, and Beatriz Sarlo. "La Argentina del centenario: Campo intelectual, vida literaria y temas ideológicos." *Hispamérica* 9 (1980).

Ardao, Arturo. "Rodó clásico." *Cuadernos de Marcha* 50 (June 1971).

Benedetti, Mario. "Hacia el esbozo verosímil de un nuevo Uruguay." *Marcha* 50 (June 18, 1971).

Camacho R., Jorge Andrés "En torno al *Ariel* de José Enrique Rodó." *Revista de la Universidad de Costa Rica* 35 (1973).

Cassou, Jean. "Renan et Rodó." *Revue de l'Amérique Latine* 5 (1923).

Charras, Julián de. "Montevideo intelectual. Con José Enrique Rodó." *Caras y Caretas* 912, 19 (March 1916).

Crema, Edoardo. "Rodó y Rubén Darío." *Revista Nacional de Cultura* 178 (1966).

Cúneo, Dardo. "Un intento de análisis de *Ariel.*" *Cuadernos Americanos* 169 (1970).

Darío, Rubén. "Cabezas. José Enrique Rodó." *Mundial* [Paris], January 1912.

Donoso, Armando. "Rodó. Evocación del espíritu de Ariel." *Nosotros* 26 (1917).

Etcheverry, José Enrique. "La revista nacional." *Número* 2 (1950).

Fernández Retamar, Roberto. "La contribución de las literaturas de la América Latina a la literatura universal en el siglo XX." *Revista de Crítica Literaria Latinoamericana* 2, 4 (1976).

Figueira, Gastón. "Conmemoración de Rodó." *Revista Interamericana de Bibliografía* 22 (1972).

Foster, David William. "Procesos de literaturización en *Ariel* de Rodó." *Explicación de textos literarios* 10 (1982); also in *Para una lectura semiótica del ensayo latino americano.* Madrid: Ediciones José Porrúa Turanzas, 1983.

Frugoni, Emilio. "Presentación de *Ariel* en Moscú." *Revista Nacional* 97 (1946).

Genta, Estrella. "José Enrique Rodó: Precursor de la psicología profunda." *Norte* 268 (1975).

Gómez-Gil, Orlando. "Panamericanismo y universalismo en Rodó." *Revista Interamericana de Bibliografía* 24 (1974).

Ibáñez, Roberto. "Noticia previa de correspondencia de José Enrique Rodó." *Fuentes* 1 (August 1961).

Junco, Alfonso. "José Enrique Rodó." *Abside: Revista de Cultura Mexicana* 35 (1971).

Le Gonidec, Bernard. "Lecture d'Ariel": La République de Rodó." *Bulletin Hispanique* 73 (1971).

Mallo, Tomás. "El Antipositivismo en México." *Cuadernos Hispanoamericanos* 390 (December 1982).

Mas, José L. "La huella de José Martí en *Ariel.*" *Hispania* 62 (1979).

Pereyra-Suárez, Esther. "José Enrique Rodó y la selección en la democracia." *Hispania* 58 (1975).

Pérez Botero, Luis. "La educación estética del hombre americano: Schiller y Rodó." *Revista Interamericana de Bibliografía* 24, 4 (1974).

Perotti, It. Eduardo. "Páginas olvidadas." *Revista Nacional; Literatura, Arte, Ciencia* 9, no. 220 (April–June 1964).

Pi, Wilfredo. "Lo vivo y permanente de *Ariel*." *Revista Nacional;
Literatura, Arte, Ciencia* 16, no. 174 (June 1953).
Real de Azúa, Carlos. "El problema de la valoración de Rodó."
Cuadernos de Marcha 1, 1967.
———. "Rodó en sus papeles." *Escritura* 3 (March 1948).
Remos, Juan J. "Rodó, apóstol de la esperanza." *Revista Nacional;
Literatura, Arte, Ciencia* 4, no. 42 (June 1941).
Retamar, R. F. "Ariel." *Revista Crítica Literaria* 2 (1976).
Rey, León. "Homenaje de Colombia a José Enrique Rodó: El
mensaje de *Ariel*." *Nivel* 113, 5 (1972).
Rodríguez, J. Pereira. "La técnica de lo poético en Rodó." *Nosotros*,
91 (1943).
Rodríguez Monegal, Emir. "Rodó y algunos coetáneos." *Número*,
1950.
———. "Sobre el anti-imperialismo de Rodó." *Revista Ibero-
americana* 38 (1972).
———. "La utopía modernista: El mito del nuevo y el viejo
mundo en Darío y Rodó." *Revista Iberoamericana* 46 (1980).
Romero, José Luis. "Ubicación de Rodó." *Marcha* 2, 1073 (1961).
Sánchez, Luis Alberto. "El Anti-Rodó." *Nosotros* 49 (1933).
Tiempo, César. "Vistazo a José Enrique Rodó." *Hispania* 39 (1956).
Torrano, Hugo. "Rodó: idealismo y cultura." *Revista Inter-
americana de Bibliografía* 24, 4 (1974).

TRANSLATIONS

Ariel. [A fragment] translated by J. F. Juge. *Revue de l'Amérique
Latine* 5 (1923).
Pages choisies. [Preface and fragments of *Ariel*] translated by Francis
de Miomandre. Paris: Librarie Félix Alcan, n.d.

DISSERTATIONS

Allen, David Harding, Jr. "Ariel and Caliban: The Turning Point
(1870–1900)." University of California, 1968.
Ariel, in Allen's view, crystalized anxieties about the United
States that Latin Americans had been feeling for the last third of
the nineteenth century. Rodó's thesis was the opposite of Sar-

miento's and was offered as an effort to combat "USA-mania" (Nordomanía). Rodó, along with Justo Sierra, José Martí, and Paul Groussac, was doubtlessly influenced by his vision of what the United States could be, as contrasted to the reality. Allen takes Rodó's metaphor as the basis for his thesis, but does not return to Rodó's contribution until his conclusion.

Berrien, William J. "Rodó: biografía y estudio crítico. University of California, Berkeley, 1937.

Langhorst, Frederick Hart. "Three Latin Americans Look at Us: The United States as Seen in the Essays of José Martí, José Enrique Rodó, and José Vasconcelos." Atlanta: Emory University, 1975.

Langhorst does not provide any new insights. He quotes Pedro Henríquez Ureña's book as an attempt to rebuild Rodó's image. He believes that Rodó "summarized and channeled a feeling about North America that had previously been either ignored or treated in a manner too random . . . to provoke general assent." Although *Ariel* is an idealistic orientation for Latin American youth, it is "a throwback to a culture foreign and inapplicable to Latin America—the culture of the Ancients."

Pereyra-Suárez, Esther. "La selección en la democracia: Rodó y el novecientos hispanoamericano." Stanford: Stanford University, 1965.

Pereyra-Suárez investigates the validity of charges of anti-democratic tendencies leveled against Rodó by critics such as Alberto Zum Felde and Luis Alberto Sánchez. Others of the *novecentista* group shared Rodó's ideal of government by a democratic—not an aristocratic—elite. Pereyra-Suárez concludes that, for better or worse, Latin America has moved away from the concept of democracy detailed in *Ariel*.

REFERENCES

Albarrán Puente, Glicerio. "Apéndice III. Bibliografía." *El pensamiento de José Enrique Rodó*. Madrid: Ediciones Cultura Hispánica, 1953.

General bibliography for Albarrán's own study, but contains references to numerous books and articles on Rodó, as well as editions of his works.

Anderson, Robert Roland. "José Enrique Rodó." *Spanish American Bibliography*. Tucson: University of Arizona Press, 1970.

Two hundred and eighty-one items; books, articles, pamphlets, special issues of journals. Best single source for periodicals. Basic Rodó library.

Benedetti, Mario. *Genio y figura de José Enrique Rodó*. Buenos Aires: Editorial Universitaria, 1966.

Skeletal list of works. Organization not clear. Entries are primarily of books, although speeches and newspaper articles are included.

Originales y documentos de José Enrique Rodó. Montevideo: Ministro de Instrucción Pública, 1947.

A summary of an exhibition of Rodó manuscripts, books, and memorabilia. A note states that the real catalogue of the exhibit, compiled by Roberto Ibáñez, would be published two weeks after the date of the exhibit, December 19, 1947.

Rodríguez Monegal, Emir. "Bibliografía crítica: fuentes impresas." *Obras completas*. Madrid: Aguilar, 1967.

Listings of general studies "containing references" and monographs on Rodó are helpful. A "second series" of entries brings bibliography more up to date. Best source for translations.

Scarone, Arturo. *Bibliografía de Rodó. El escritor. Las obras. La crítica*. Two volumes. Prologue by Ariosto D. González. Montevideo: Imprenta Nacional, 1930.

Volume 1 catalogues Rodó's writings, 1,069 entries. González's prologue reviews the criticism of Rodó's work. Scarone writes that "this is still another homage to Rodó [expressing] my admiration and respect, and—why not admit it—my patriotic and Americanist emotions." Volume 2 contains 2,039 entries of "Criticism on the Life and Work of Rodó," organized by chronological periods. Interesting photographs and memorabilia. The obvious limitation is its date of publication. Essential for Rodó library.

Welch, Thomas L. *Bibliografía de la literatura uruguaya*. Washington: Biblioteca Colón, 1985.

The Biblioteca Colón is the library of the Organization of

American States, and this valuable volume is part of its continuing effort to "contribute to the increased awareness of the literature of Latin America." The bibliography consists of 9,329 titles, all books or *separata*. Essential for Rodó library.

ACKNOWLEDGMENT

I am grateful to Don Kuderer for assisting me in gathering the items for this bibliography.

Index

Ortega y Gasset, José, 23, 110
otium, 47, 48, 79

Parnassianism, 13, 64
Pascal, Blaise, 79, 110
Paul, St., 52, 65
perfectionism, 41
pessimism, 34, 38–39
Peter, St., 53
Philadelphia, 86
Philippi, 53
Phoenicians, 94
pioneers, 75
Piraeus, 92
Plato, 37, 52, 88, 98, 110, 111
plutocracy, 84
Poe, Edgar Allan, 17, 77–78, 81, 82,
  104, 110
politics, 23–24, 72. *See also*
  governing
polytheism, 19–20
Pompey, 109
positivism, 63, 80, 88–89, 105, 107,
  111, 113
Positivists, 43, 79
potentiality, 66
Prometheus, 63
prosperity, 79, 83–84
Prospero, 31, 32, 99, 110, 112
Prudhomme, 61–62, 109, 111
public life, 84
Puritanism, 52, 75, 76, 80, 81–82,
  84
Pylos, 45
Pythagoras, 56, 111

quality vs. numbers, 59–61, 64, 84,
  91–92
Quinet, Edgard, 91, 95, 111

realism, 106
reason, 31

religion, 76, 83. *See also*
  Christianity
Renaissance, 52
Renan, Joseph Ernest, 33, 36, 41,
  51, 57–58, 63–64, 65, 88, 106, 111
responsibility, 68
Rivadavia, Bernardino, 93, 111
Rod, Edouard, 17, 37, 111
Romanticism, 37, 104, 105, 107,
  108, 109
Rome, 80, 85, 86
Roosevelt, Theodore, 13
Rosas, Juan Manuel de, 15, 111
Rosenkrantz, Karl, 54, 111
Rousseau, Jean-Jacques, 62, 110,
  112

Saint-Victor, Paul de, 88, 112
Sandinistas, 25
Santa Anna, Antonio López de, 15,
  112
Sarmiento, Domingo Faustino, 17,
  93, 112
Schiller, Friedrich von, 49, 112
Scholasticism, 112
Schopenhauer, Arthur, 106
science, 65, 68–69, 82. *See also*
  natural science
Scythians, 93
self, 45–48
selflessness, 31, 41, 57, 83, 94
Semiramis, Queen, 92
Seneca, Lucius Annaeus, 54, 112
Shakespeare, William, 17, 31, 98,
  99, 112
Sidon, 93
skepticism, 38–39
Solon, 35, 112
Somoza, Anastasio, 25
sorrow, 39
soul, 33, 50–51
Southern Cross, 101
Sparta, 73

specialization, 42–43
Spencer, Herbert, 78–79, 90, 112
spirit, 37, 44–45
State, the, 66
Statue of Liberty, 87, 104
Stoicism, 113
Stoics, 36, 38, 47–48, 51, 105
success, 84
Sunium, 98
superiority, natural, 65–67, 68, 69–70, 86
superman, 68, 77, 110
Surrealists, 104
survival. *See* evolution
Symbolism, 13
Syrius, 100

Taine, Hippolyte, 53, 63–64, 80, 85, 95, 104, 113
Tarde, Gabriel, 18, 74, 113
Tempest, The, 31, 112
Tennyson, Alfred Lord, 92, 108
Thackeray, William Makepeace, 72, 113
Thessaly, 52, 53
Thomas à Kempis, 84
Thomism, 20, 113
Thoreau, Henry David, 105
thought, 94
Titania, 62
Tocqueville, Alexis de, 67, 74, 82, 83, 113
Tower of Babel, 92
Transcendentalism, 104, 105
Transtevere, 36
truth, 82
Tuscany, 108
Tyre, 93

Uhland, Johann Ludwig, 46, 113
Ultima Thule, 47
urbanism, 27. *See also* city
USA: attributes and deficits of,

22–23, 74–90; education in, 75; expansion of democracy by, 24–26; good taste in, 81; idealism in, 76; mediocrity in, 82; morality in, 83–84; as utilitarian, 71, 76, 85; western, 85–86
utilitarianism, 109; and aestheticism, 57; and beauty, 55–56; and democracy, 57–70; and education, 41; and egalitarianism, 63; and humanity, 91; and idealism, 56–57, 78–79, 88–89; as limited, 44–45; and mediocrity, 70–71; and morality, 83; and natural science, 57; and public life, 84; and selflessness, 57; in USA, 71, 76, 85; value of, 87–88

Vallejo, César, 20, 113
Virginia, 85, 86
virtue, 50, 52, 83. *See also* morality
vulgarity, 51, 61, 62, 63

Walker, William, 16
war, 48
Ward, Mrs. Humphrey, 37
Weber, Max, 19
Whitman, Walt, 13, 17
work. *See* labor
worldliness, 36
Wyzewa, Téodor de, 17, 37

Yankee heritage, 85, 86
youth: attributes of, 33, 34–35, 36; and cities, 93–94; and future, 94–95, 96, 98; and Plato, 37

Zeno, 48, 105, 113
Zola, Émile Edouard Charles Antoine, 111
zoocracy, 62

[156]

Printed in the USA
CPSIA information can be obtained
at www.ICGtesting.com
JSHW021112310723
45663JS00002B/30